Jesus and ...

HOW GOD WORKS THROUGH ORDINARY PEOPLE

&

How God
works through
ordinary people

Jesus and ...

Robert Fergusson

JESUS AND …
Published by David C Cook
4050 Lee Vance Drive
Colorado Springs, CO 80918 U.S.A.

Integrity Music Limited, a Division of David C Cook
Brighton, East Sussex BN1 2RE, England

DAVID C COOK®, the graphic circle C logo and related marks are registered trademarks of David C Cook.

All rights reserved. Except for brief excerpts for review purposes, no part of this book may be reproduced or used in any form without written permission from the publisher.

Unless otherwise indicated, all Scripture quotations are from the Holy Bible, New International Version®, NIV®. Copyright © 1973, 2011 by Biblica, Inc.™ Used by permission of Zondervan. All rights reserved worldwide. www.zondervan.com. The "NIV" and "New International Version" are trademarks registered in the United States Patent and Trademark Office by Biblica, Inc.™

LCCN on file with the Library of Congress
ISBN 978-0-8307-9003-6
eISBN 978-0-8307-9004-3

© 2023, 2024 Robert Fergusson, published by David C Cook in association with Hillsong Music & Resources, LLC
First published in Australia by City & Vine, ISBN 978-1-922411-45-7.

Cover Design: Kevin Villanueva
Internal Design: Abrupt Media

Printed in the United States of America
First Edition 2023

1 2 3 4 5 6 7 8 9 10

CONTENTS

13/ Volume One: PREFACE

29/ Jesus and ... INTRODUCTION

33/ Chapter One: JESUS, ZECHARIAH, ELIZABETH, AND JOHN
—Finding hope for your family

53/ Chapter Two: JESUS AND ANNA
   Finding significance in the ordinary

77/ Chapter Three: JESUS AND JOHN THE BAPTIST
   Finding purpose in life

107/ Chapter Four: JESUS AND THE MAN WITH LEPROSY
   Finding acceptance and healing

131/ Chapter Five: JESUS AND THE CENTURION
   Finding faith in a time of unbelief

155/ CONCLUSION

He includes us in His story of salvation. We become partners and coworkers with Him, each with a part to play, each with an assigned task.

13
Volume One

PREFACE

&

God's methodology is a Person.

When God wanted to save the world, to reconcile the world to Himself, He sent His Son, the Lord Jesus Christ. He didn't send a guidebook, or a manual for living—He sent a Person. Someone who could reveal what God was like and tell us His story. Someone who would face our challenges and overcome them. Someone who would live among us and to whom we could relate.

The Word became flesh and made his dwelling among us. We have seen his glory, the glory of the one and only Son, who came from the Father, full of grace and truth.
(John 1:14).

Christianity is not about rules and regulations, it is about a relationship with God through His Son, the Lord Jesus Christ. If we want to know God the Father, we can do so through the life of His Son. If we want to be reconciled with God the Father, we can do so through the accomplishments of His Son. We can receive forgiveness, hope, and empowerment for life through His death, resurrection, and ascension. Jesus Christ is our Go-Between, the Mediator of a new and better way of living.

Preface

We can receive forgiveness, hope, and empowerment for life through His death, resurrection, and ascension.

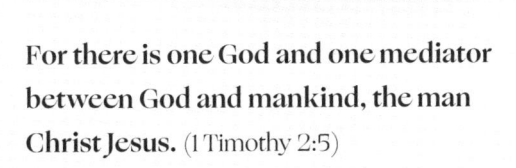

For there is one God and one mediator between God and mankind, the man **Christ Jesus.** (1 Timothy 2:5)

Jesus and ...

> We become partners and coworkers with Him, each with a part to play, each with an assigned task.

Jesus Christ is the subject of this book—hence the title. But this is where God's story of salvation becomes even more extraordinary. God's methodology is not just a Person. God's methodology is people—hence the "and" in the title.

God doesn't just save us, He calls us. He gives us a purpose in life. He includes us in His story of salvation. We become partners and coworkers with Him, each with a part to play, each with an assigned task.

What, after all, is Apollos? And what is Paul? Only servants, through whom you came to believe—as the Lord has assigned to each his task ... For we are coworkers in God's service; you are God's field, God's building.
(1 Corinthians 3:5, 9)

Both Apollos and Paul had equal value. They were both reconciled to God through the grace of the Lord Jesus Christ. But then, remarkably, God chose to empower and equip them for His service. He gave each of them a different task, and although their roles in God's field were *distinct*—one planted while the other watered—both roles were equally significant and valuable. Both Apollos and Paul were not only reconciled with God, but were also given a ministry of reconciliation. They became God's representatives, His ambassadors.

We are therefore Christ's ambassadors, as though God were making his appeal through us. We implore you on Christ's behalf: Be reconciled to God.
(2 Corinthians 5:20)

This is the heart of this book. God uses people to fulfill His purpose on earth. In His sovereignty and grace, He chooses ordinary, flawed people like you and me. He places value on our lives and gives us a part to play in His kingdom. Of course we have nothing to boast about, because we are recipients of grace—but nonetheless, our story matters. Your story matters.

God doesn't just save us—He calls us.

Jesus and ...

But there is a potential danger in this line of thought.

In his book *The Screwtape Letters*, the author C. S. Lewis imagines a conversation between an experienced demon (Screwtape) and his apprentice (Wormwood). Screwtape advises Wormwood in the effective temptation of Christians. The book highlights how easy it is to become a victim of deception.

In one memorable passage, Lewis introduces the concept of "Christianity And," the idea that we can lose our focus on truth by adding our own opinions.

> What we want, if men become Christians at all, is to keep them in the state of mind I call "Christianity And." You know—Christianity and the Crisis, Christianity and the New Psychology, Christianity and Psychical Research, Christianity and Vegetarianism, Christianity and Spelling Reform. If they must be Christians let them at least be Christians with a difference. Substitute for the faith itself some Fashion with a Christian colouring.[1]
> (C. S. Lewis)

> We mustn't add our modern concerns, opinions, or controversies to His Name. He stands alone.

The dangers and variations of this idea are obvious—and endless. And the reason I mention them is that I don't want us to fall into the same trap with the title of this series, "Jesus and …"

Jesus Christ is self-sufficient. He is Truth. We mustn't add our modern concerns, opinions, or controversies to His Name. He stands alone. Jesus doesn't need an "and." So why have I given this series of books the title "Jesus and …"? Because, as I have explained, God sent a Person to save the world and uses people to serve the world. God's methodology is a Person and people.

God's plan is to make much of the man, far more of him than of anything else. Men are God's method. The Church is looking for better methods; God is looking for better men.[2] (E. M. Bounds)

Of course we know that God cannot be defined by, or limited to, a methodology. And we also know that God can and does act on His own. But throughout history, it is evident that He often uses people to fulfill His purpose. This idea has been hugely influential in my life.

In 1985, I was in a meeting in which the Sri-Lankan prophet Colton Wickramaratne was preaching. Suddenly he pointed at me and said, "God's method is a man, and you are that man." As you can imagine, I was shocked and slightly embarrassed, but his statement sparked my curiosity. Are people God's methodology, and could I be one of those people? I discovered later that the statement was a ministry mantra for him; nonetheless, it became a defining moment for me. Perhaps this book can help it to become one for you as well.

The story of the early church is filled with extraordinary examples of God's resolve to partner with ordinary people like you and me. Take for example the conversion of Saul, who later became Paul the apostle. We often assume he had a private encounter

> God's method is a man or woman, and you can be that person for God.³
> (Colton Wickramaratne)

with Jesus on the road to Damascus. But there are many others involved in the story: his companions who witnessed the event, the man who prayed for him, and the owner of the house in Damascus where his sight was restored. Each of them had a part to play. But why were they necessary? Why didn't God cut out the middlemen?

The Lord told him, "Go to the house of Judas on Straight Street and ask for a man from Tarsus named Saul, for he is praying. In a vision he has seen a man named Ananias come and place his hands on him to restore his sight."

(Acts 9:11-12)

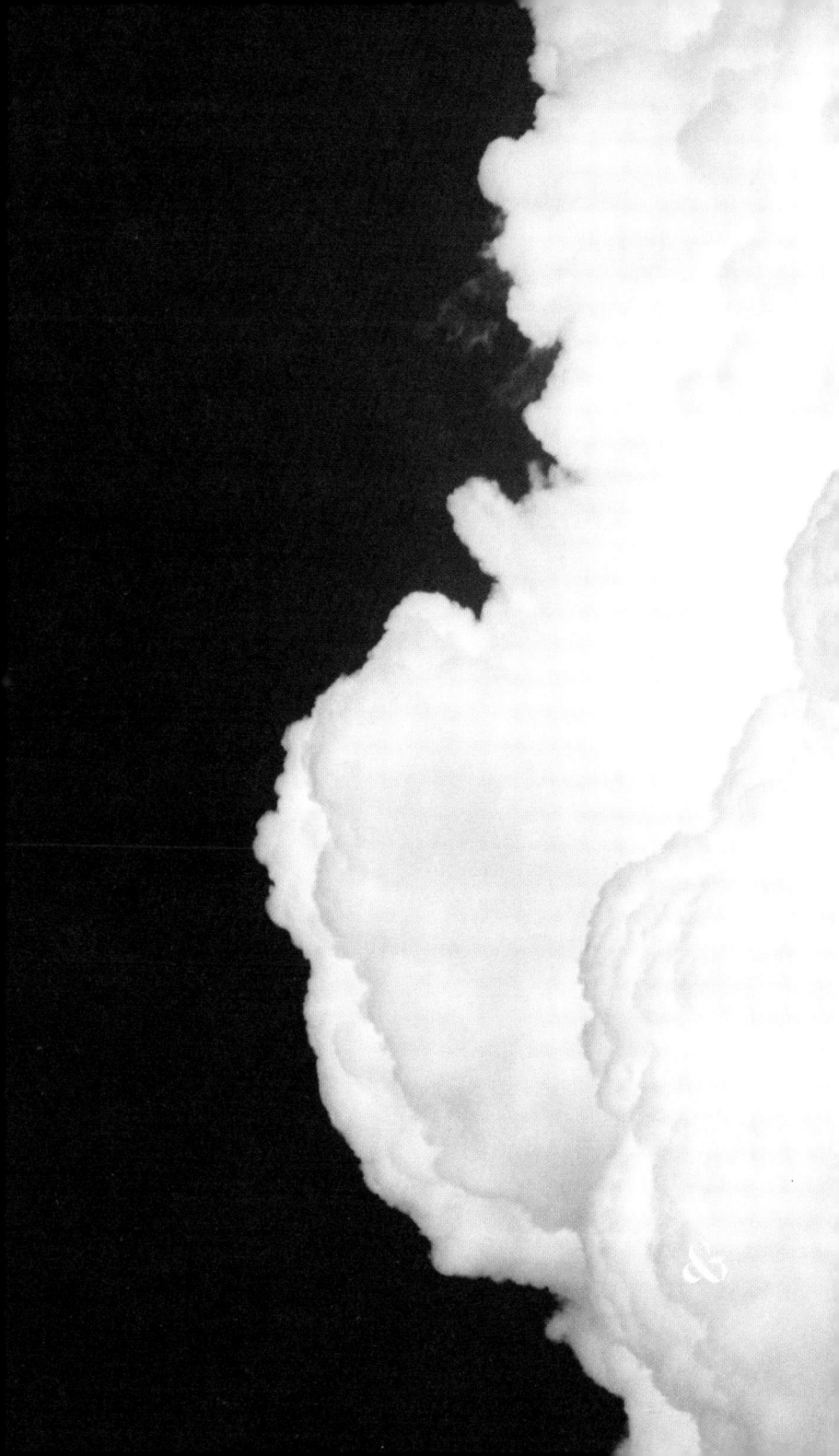

The same situation occurs in the story of Cornelius's conversion in the following chapter. In this case, an angel appears to Cornelius in his home. Once again, Luke, the author of the book of Acts, records the people involved: the messengers, Peter, and Simon the tanner.

Now send men to Joppa to bring back a man named Simon who is called Peter. He is staying with Simon the tanner, whose house is by the sea. (Acts 10:5-6)

But why did God involve them in the story? Why didn't the angel suffice? It seems that God wants to use people. Hence the title of this series. Jesus and …

Jesus and people.

The story of Israel also illustrates our theme. For example, when God wanted to save Israel from exile, He looked for a person through whom He could carry out His plan. The unlikely person He chose was Cyrus, a Persian king.

From the east I summon a bird of prey; from a far-off land, a man to fulfill my purpose. What I have said, that I will bring about; what I have planned, that I will do. (Isaiah 46:11)

In the New Testament, the gospel writers reveal some equally unlikely people through whom God fulfilled His purpose. Luke,

Preface

for instance, records numerous stories of improbable men and women with whom Jesus chose to work. They included tax collectors and fishermen; centurions and servants; the wealthy and the poor; the named and the unnamed. These ordinary people are the subjects of this book. Their stories contain valuable lessons for each one of us. Maybe God could use us as He did them? Jesus and …

Jesus and you.

Every story contains wisdom for our lives— for your life.

29
Jesus and …

INTRODUCTION

&

The Bible is a storybook.

It is the story of God's salvation. God is both the Author and the central Character. But the Bible also contains other stories, including the story of Israel, and the story of the early church. And within these stories are numerous ordinary characters, like you and me, who found their sub-plot in God's story.

This book is about some of those people and what we can learn from their lives.

Each story is taken from the book of Luke. The stories that he recorded in his gospel were passed on to him by eyewitnesses of the events which he wanted to share. Every story contains wisdom for our lives—for your life. I have chosen these five stories because they have profoundly impacted my life and I believe can also impact yours.

Introduction

Many have undertaken to draw up an account of the things that have been fulfilled among us, just as they were handed down to us by those who from the first were eyewitnesses and servants of the word. (Luke 1:1-2)

The five stories in this book are about a variety of people in very different settings to ours—yet the challenges they faced, and the aspirations they had, are remarkably similar. They wanted the best for their family, to make a difference in their world and to live healthy and fulfilling lives.

In the century after Luke, one of the great Christian writers declared that he preferred living testimony to writings. You can't tell where a book has come from, but you can look a witnesses in the eye, and use your judgement about whether to trust them.[4] (Tom Wright)

As these living testimonies are worth studying in greater depth than I am able to do on these pages, I have included a number of questions at the end of each chapter to help you do exactly that.

My hope is that these five stories will change your life as much as they have changed mine.

Jesus Christ came to save ordinary people like Zechariah and Elizabeth—like you and me.

33

Chapter One

JESUS AND ZECHARIAH, ELIZABETH, AND JOHN

Finding hope for your family

&

Jesus and ...

My family is flawed and yet called.

After an extensive search of my family history, I discovered that several of my ancestors were Christian ministers. But on the other hand, it seems some were criminals. One eighteenth-century ancestor was on the run from the authorities in Scotland because of "his rather free use of his dirk ..." Another, in the nineteenth century, wrote that his "wretched wife, after having involved me greatly in debt, is now living in France in the most profligate and depraved manner." Yet despite this rather mixed backstory, I still have immense hope for my family.

How would you describe your family? Is it large or small, together or separated, broken or blended? Whatever it is like, each one of you is part of some sort of family. And whether you can explain it or not, you have an aspiration for it. Maybe you want it healed or perhaps you want it to fulfill its potential. Either way, like me, you have a desire for your family—some sort of a dream ... a hope.

Tragically, we live in a fallen and complicated world. It's filled with conflict, insecurity, and anxiety. Some couples are even frightened to have children because of this uncertain future. It's very easy to lose hope for our family in these circumstances. Thankfully, God is a God of hope, and the Bible is filled with stories of hope. These stories have the power to change the course of our lives. One of these is found in the first chapter of the book of Luke.

Luke starts his gospel with an old priest and his childless wife. To begin the story of Jesus Christ, the King of Kings, with the doubts and concerns of two of His servants, seems a very curious decision. Yet this strange introduction sets the scene for the gospel. Jesus Christ came to save ordinary people like Zechariah and Elizabeth—like you and me.

In the time of Herod king of Judea there was a priest named Zechariah, who belonged to the priestly division of Abijah; his wife Elizabeth was also a descendant of Aaron. Both of them were righteous in the sight of God, observing all the Lord's commands and decrees blamelessly. But they were childless because Elizabeth was not able to conceive, and they were both very old. (Luke 1:5-7)

The narrative continues with the angel Gabriel appearing to Zechariah while he is serving in the temple. The angel promises him that his wife Elizabeth will bear a son, who is to be named John. Luke's gospel is filled with these unexpected acts of grace. This favored family unit has a great deal to teach us about God's plans for our families.

Then an angel of the Lord appeared to him, standing at the right side of the altar of incense. When Zechariah saw him, he was startled and was gripped with fear. But the angel said to him: "Do not be afraid, Zechariah; your prayer has been heard. Your wife Elizabeth will bear you a son, and you are to call him John." (Luke 1:11-13)

Zechariah, like many of us, failed to believe the promise of God. As a result, he was unable to speak until the promise was fulfilled. When it came time to name the child, he made it clear to everyone present that the boy would be called John. As soon as he had done so, his mouth was opened, and he began to praise God.

On the eighth day they came to circumcise the child, and they were going to name him after his father Zechariah, but his mother spoke up and said, "No! He is to be called John." They said to her, "There is no one among your relatives who has that name." Then they made signs to his father, to find out what he would like to name the child. He asked for a writing tablet, and to everyone's astonishment he wrote, "His name is John." (Luke 1:59-63)

Who was this child? And what was so significant about his name?

Zechariah, Elizabeth, and John

But the angel said to him: "Do not be afraid, Zechariah; your prayer has been heard."

(Luke 1:13)

Jesus and ...

What's in a name?

In his play *Romeo and Juliet*, William Shakespeare posed the question, "What's in a name?"[5] It is a pertinent question in the play because the fates of his protagonists were determined by their surnames. But what about real life? Can our names describe our destiny?

Before our first daughter was born, my wife and I had decided on her name. She was going to be called Natasha. But when we saw her, we immediately knew her name was Catherine. The name "Catherine" is derived from the Greek word that means "pure." It's a name that she has carried well. Years later I discovered two godly and influential women in our family history with the same name and the same spelling. Was this purely coincidence, or did God direct the choice of her name?

In the Bible, names often have much greater significance than we give them today. The Names of God, for instance, describe His eternal character as well as His covenant with His people. And throughout the Bible, names are given, or changed, to reflect a change of fortunes. Abraham (see Genesis 17:5) and Peter (see John 1:42) are good examples. Occasionally names have a prophetic significance as they did in the names of the prophet Isaiah and his family.

Isaiah prophesied in the eighth century (BC), at a critical time in Israel's history. He foretold, among other things, that the people of God were about to be exiled; that God would rescue them; and that they would return to their homeland. His name, and the names of his sons, described this prophetic message.

One of his sons was named Maher-Shalal-Hash-Baz (and you thought modern names were strange!), which literally means "Quick to the plunder and swift to the spoil" and referred to Israel's imminent exile (see Isaiah 8:1–4). Another son was named Shear-Jashub, which means "a remnant will return" (see Isaiah 7:3 and Isaiah 10:21). And Isaiah's name means "God is your salvation" (see Isaiah 12:2). So, together, the names of this prophetic family proclaimed to Israel, "You will be exiled, but God is your salvation, and a remnant will return."

Isaiah and his family embodied his prophetic message.

Here am I, and the children the LORD has given me. We are signs and symbols in Israel from the LORD Almighty, who dwells on Mount Zion. (Isaiah 8:18)

Jesus and ...

A prophetic family

But what does Isaiah's family have to do with Zechariah? Well, even though Zechariah was a simple priest, he had a number of things in common with his more illustrious forebear. First, he could and did prophesy. Second, he foresaw the coming Messiah (even if his foresight was a little less impressive than Isaiah's). And third, he also had a prophetic family. This is revealed when Zechariah prophesied after his speech was restored, and he had named his son.

> His father Zechariah was filled with the Holy Spirit and prophesied: "Praise be to the Lord, the God of Israel, because he has come to his people and redeemed them. He has raised up a horn of salvation for us in the house of his servant David (as he said through his holy prophets of long ago), salvation from our enemies and from the hand of all who hate us—to show mercy to our ancestors and to remember his holy covenant, the oath he swore to our father Abraham: to rescue us from the hand of our enemies, and to enable us to serve him without fear in holiness and righteousness before him all our days. (Luke 1:67-75)

In this prophecy, Zechariah confesses three truths about God and His people: God remembered His covenant to save them; He swore an oath to bless them; and He showed grace to rescue them. Once again, the prophet and his family embodied this three-part message. "Zechariah" means "The Lord remembers"; "Elizabeth" means, "the oath of God"; and "John" means "the favour or grace of God."

But this prophetic family not only described the blessing they themselves had received, but they also foreshadowed the salvation that we can all receive.

The future ministry of their son John, who became John the Baptist, prepared the way for Jesus Christ. In Jesus Christ, the same three-fold message would be revealed—for us all. God remembers His covenant (see Hebrews 12:22–24); God swears an oath to bless us (see Hebrews 6:13–20); and God makes grace and favor available for each one of us (see Hebrews 4:16).

The prophetic families of Isaiah and Zechariah can give hope for all of our families. Both families lived in immensely difficult times. The people of God were under threat. But both families embodied God's faithfulness. And God's word and Spirit sustained them. Their example and witness can be our pattern—your pattern.

To some degree, I have modeled my family on theirs. And when my family has faced battles, uncertainties, and threats, I have confessed the promises of God over each one of them, as both Isaiah and Zechariah did. May I encourage you to do the same.

> "As for me, this is my covenant with them," says the LORD.
> "My Spirit, who is on you, will not depart from you, and my words that I have put in your mouth will always be on your lips, on the lips of your children and on the lips of their descendants—from this time on and forever," says the LORD.
>
> (Isaiah 59:21)

Warnings and examples

The family of this simple priest proclaimed, embodied, and foretold the gospel. Their entire life and ministry pointed toward the Lord Jesus Christ. But what else can we learn from Zechariah's prophetic family?

First, we should be encouraged that God saw Zechariah and Elizabeth in their distress. Luke describes them as "not able to conceive" and "very old." They not only lived with the pain of childlessness but also with the possibility of poverty. They had no children to support them in their later years. But God saw their situation, answered their prayers, and blessed them with a child. God delights in doing the impossible. What God did for them He can do for us.

Jesus and ...

> **But the angel said to him: "Do not be afraid, Zechariah; your prayer has been heard. Your wife Elizabeth will bear you a son, and you are to call him John. He will be a joy and delight to you, and many will rejoice because of his birth."** (Luke 1:13-14)

However, God didn't just have a personal blessing for Zechariah, Elizabeth, and John; He had a plan for the family as a whole. As we have seen, each of them had an individual word to share in God's message of salvation, and yet their family completed the sentence. Each of them had a personal story, and yet they were part of a larger family narrative.

Throughout Luke's writing (he wrote the Acts of the Apostles as well as his gospel), he tells stories about entire households who find salvation. For example, Lydia (see Acts 16:15), the Philippian jailer (see Acts 16:31), and Crispus (see Acts 18:8) all became believers with their families. And Cornelius was told by an angel that the gospel would bring salvation to his entire family (see Acts 11:13–14). Although his salvation was personal, his conversion opened the door to his household. The same can be true for you and me.

> **He told us how he had seen an angel appear in his house and say, "Send to Joppa for Simon who is called Peter. He will bring you a message through which you and all your household will be saved."** (Acts 11:13-14)

I have a friend whose family were unbelievers. However, his uncle, who was in a coma, was miraculously healed through the prayers of a stranger. The transformation was so remarkable that the uncle and his brothers all became Christians. Within about two weeks, thirty-seven members of the family had also become believers. Many of them became ministers. Like the stories of Zechariah and Cornelius, one supernatural encounter impacted the entire family.

But as I have already noted, Zechariah's story was not all positive. He failed to believe the good news about the upcoming birth of his son. He wasn't even convinced by the presence of an angel! The people in the Bible are not without fault. Their flaws exemplify human frailty—and mirror our own failings. Their stories act as warnings. After all, how many times have we failed to believe the promises of God?

Zechariah asked the angel, "How can I be sure of this? I am an old man and my wife is well along in years." The angel said to him, "I am Gabriel. I stand in the presence of God, and I have been sent to speak to you and to tell you this good news." (Luke 1:18-19)

But alongside the warnings, the Bible always provides positive examples. We are constantly encouraged to heed the warnings and follow the examples. Mary, Elizabeth's relative, was also visited by an angel and was also promised a son, but unlike

Zechariah, she believed. Where Zechariah exemplified doubt, Mary personified faith. When he wondered if the miracle could happen, she wondered how it would happen.

"How will this be," Mary asked the angel, "since I am a virgin?" The angel answered, "The Holy Spirit will come on you, and the power of the Most High will overshadow you. So the holy one to be born will be called the Son of God. Even Elizabeth your relative is going to have a child in her old age, and she who was said to be unable to conceive is in her sixth month. For no word from God will ever fail." "I am the Lord's servant," Mary answered. "May your word to me be fulfilled." Then the angel left her.

(Luke 1:34-38)

What these stories teach us is that when God makes a promise, He will fulfill it, and if He speaks to us, it is better for us if we believe it. We may never have been visited by an angel, but God has made numerous promises about our future in His Word. Are we prepared to learn from Mary's example and Zechariah's warning and take God at His word?

Zechariah, Elizabeth, and John

I wonder what final advice Zechariah and Elizabeth would give us once they had learned from their experiences. I suspect they might tell us that God has His own timeframe, and that we should trust Him. They waited a long time for their first child. And after many years of seemingly unanswered prayer, they finally received their miracle. John arrived just at the right time, both for them and for us.

> **And now you will be silent and not able to speak until the day this happens, because you did not believe my words, which will come true at their appointed time.**
>
> (Luke 1:20)

Jesus and ...

When I read the stories of people like Zechariah in the Bible, I see my life in theirs. I recognize my own doubts and dreams, my own faith and frailties. But I also see them as potential mentors. I look for counsel in their experiences. If I share their situation, I attempt to discern God's wisdom. Perhaps God's word to them is also God's word to me—or to you.

Jesus and us

Zechariah grasped some foundational truths. Truths that we also need to grasp if we are going to receive all that God has for us and our families. Despite his initial doubts, he learned to trust God. He began to believe that God's plans for his family were more wonderful than he could have possibly imagined. He prophesied over his son and spoke of a hope-filled future. And he praised God before the promises were fulfilled and the hope realized.

His father Zechariah was filled with the Holy Spirit and prophesied: "Praise be to the Lord, the God of Israel, because he has come to his people and redeemed them. He has raised up a horn of salvation for us in the house of his servant David (as he said through his holy prophets of long ago)." (Luke 1:67-70)

The story of Zechariah teaches us that God uses the most unlikely of people, and that He has good news for each one of us—if only we would believe it. And that good news extends to our whole family—if only we would accept it.

Praise be to the Lord, the God of Israel, because he has come to his people and redeemed them.

(Luke 1:68)

QUESTIONS TO CONSIDER

1. Zechariah's family had a prophetic impact on the community (Luke 1:65-66). In what ways can modern families impact their communities?

2. The book of Acts records that entire families became believers (Acts 16:13-15; Acts 16:25-34; Acts 18:8). Have you encountered families with a similar story? What have you learned from them?

3. The church is described as God's family (Hebrews 2:11; Galatians 6:10). In what ways can the church model a healthy family to the world?

4. Zechariah and Elizabeth's situation seemed impossible and yet God answered their prayers (Luke 1:7; Luke 1:13; Luke 1:24-25). In what areas are you believing God for the impossible?

5. Zechariah and Mary responded in different ways to the angel's message (Luke 1:18-19; Luke 1:34-38). Which response is closest to the way in which you respond to God's promises? What can you learn from their reactions?

Zechariah, Elizabeth, and John

6. Elizabeth and Mary received different reactions to their pregnancies (Luke 1:58; Matthew 1:18-19). What do you think Zechariah and Elizabeth's hospitality meant to Mary (Luke 1:39-45)?

7. Zechariah's prophecy (Luke 1:68-79) fulfilled several Old Testament prophetic promises (Genesis 22:16-18; Isaiah 9:2; Jeremiah 23:5; Micah 7:20; Malachi 3:1; Malachi 4:2). How do you think the people who heard it might have responded?

8. Zechariah and Elizabeth discovered that God's timing was perfect and yet different to theirs (Luke 1:5-17). What have you learned about God's timing and what does submission to God's timing look like in your life?

9. God had an amazing plan for Zechariah and his family (Luke 1:11-17). What has God promised you about your family?

10. What has been your main takeaway from this chapter? What lessons have you learned which you can apply to your life today?

You did not choose me, but I chose you and appointed you so that you might go and bear fruit—fruit that will last.

(John 15:16)

53
Chapter Two

JESUS AND ANNA

Finding significance
in the ordinary

&

Jesus and ...

Many years ago, when I was a student at university in England, I volunteered to help with a building project in the local church I attended.

As I am not a skilled worker, I was placed in a line of people who were passing bricks to the builders. It was mundane, repetitive, but necessary work. Two sisters, Gladys and Ethel, worked alongside me all day. They were both in their eighties. Their simple and unheralded contribution had a profound effect on me. Why do I remember this event so vividly? And what does their story have to do with you?

Every one of us is looking for significance in life. We want to know we have made a difference—that we are valuable to the community. Sadly, when we observe people who we think are more successful than we are (perhaps because they have a better education, a bigger house, or a more expensive car), we can feel insignificant—even worthless. And sometimes these same high achievers boast of their successes and criticize what they see as our failings, and so we feel devalued. Tragically, many of the people who devalue us are our friends, our teachers—even our parents. So how do you respond to this criticism?

There is nothing wrong with temporal success. In fact, it is part of God's promise of a blessed life and is often simply the outcome of our good choices (see Joshua 1:8). However, when Jesus Christ taught His disciples, He didn't appoint them to be successful. He appointed them to be fruitful. And as we know, fruit is a product of connection, not choice. And the eternal fruit we produce by being connected to Jesus Christ is not houses and cars, but love and kindness.

You did not choose me, but I chose you and appointed you so that you might go and bear fruit—fruit that will last—and so that whatever you ask in my name the Father will give you. This is my command: Love each other. (John 15:16–17)

Jesus and ...

My friends Gladys and Ethel may not have been perceived as successful, and yet they were wonderfully fruitful. And the fruit of their kindness contained seeds that not only impacted me but also continue to bear fruit long after their passing. Their simple act of service in a car park in England was the outcome of a profound and intimate faith in the Lord Jesus Christ. They found significance in the ordinary.

You either make people a little better or leave them a little worse. You define your faith and moral posture in the ordinary stuff of your daily routine.[6] (Frederick Buechner)

It is often these mundane actions by unlikely people that are the most significant stories in the kingdom of God. The Gospels are filled with these stories, and especially in Luke's gospel, many of them include women. One of these involves an elderly woman named Anna, who gave thanks. Of all the stories Luke heard and researched, why did he record this one? And what can we learn from these few lines?

There was also a prophet, Anna, the daughter of Penuel, of the tribe of Asher. She was very old; she had lived with her husband seven years after her marriage, and then was a widow until she was eighty-four. She never left the temple but worshiped night and day, fasting and praying. Coming up to them at that very moment, she gave thanks to God and spoke about the child to all who were looking forward to the redemption of Jerusalem. (Luke 2:36-38)

> God included her story in His.
> Perhaps her seemingly unhistoric
> story is much more significant
> than we first imagined?

On first glance, this story seems completely arbitrary—almost irrelevant. If this were a scene in a modern movie, it almost certainly would have ended up on the cutting room floor. Anna would have been relegated to the large group of unknown actors whose small contribution failed to take the story forward. But God included her story in His. Perhaps her seemingly unhistoric story is much more significant than we first imagined? Maybe it contains truths that are highly prized by God—truths that we also need to value.

Setting the scene

The temple where Anna spent her days was a hive of activity. It's difficult for us to imagine the sights and smells with which she was so familiar. Numerous priests and temple servants, some in richly ornamented robes, said fervent prayers and made daily offerings. In the temple courts, animals were bought and sold for the proscribed sacrifices, and pilgrims exchanged their currency for the required temple coinage. Apart from the noise of the animals and the visitors, there must have been a pungent atmosphere of sacred incense, dove dung, and spilled blood.

It was into this scene that Mary and Joseph came to fulfill the requirements of the law. Perhaps for simple convenience, it seems that two separate ceremonies were involved in their visit—the presentation of the child (see Numbers 18:15–16) and the purification of the mother (see Leviticus 12:6–8). In the case of the first ceremony, as Jesus was the firstborn and consequently belonged to the Lord, His parents were required to pay the redemption price of five shekels. Although the payment is not mentioned, it is assumed.

> **When the time came for the purification rites required by the Law of Moses, Joseph and Mary took him to Jerusalem to present him to the Lord (as it is written in the Law of the Lord, "Every firstborn male is to be consecrated to the Lord"), and to offer a sacrifice in keeping with what is said in the Law of the Lord: "a pair of doves or two young pigeons."** (Luke 2:22–24)

The second ceremony involved the purification of Mary, who would have been considered unclean after the birth of her child. Although this ceremony required the sacrifice of a lamb and a dove, there was a special dispensation for those who couldn't afford a lamb. Mary's offering of two young pigeons was an indicator of her financial position. Any observant people in the temple would have identified Mary and Joseph, and the child they carried, as a poor but faithful family. However, there were two people present that day who had greater perception—Simeon and Anna.

Both Simeon and Anna recognized Jesus as their long-awaited Messiah. It was a life-changing meeting. The One they saw as greater than the temple in which they served transformed their lives in one brief encounter. Although Luke gives a few more details about Simeon, the story of Anna is no less meaningful. Amid the troubles of her nation and the challenges of her life, she was able to perceive the hope of a future redemption. What was it about this woman that enabled her to see beyond the normal routines of her day?

Jesus and ...

Hidden qualities

Luke records little of Anna's story, and yet what he does write is highly significant. He describes her as a prophet. This was a profound claim in a nation with few recorded prophetesses—the Talmud only identifies seven. But the description is even more noteworthy because of the time in which she lived. God had been strangely silent since the last of the Old Testament prophets, but now, at this momentous time in history, He raised up another—someone who would recognize His Son.

In the temple that day, there were priests and pilgrims, merchants and mothers, guards and gatekeepers—all busy with their duties and affairs and distracted by the demands of their lives. But Anna was not preoccupied. She was present and aware. Like the wise before her, she understood the times. She knew what God was doing and also what we should do.

Since it was customary for the king to consult experts in matters of law and justice, he spoke with the wise men who understood the times. (Esther 1:13)

In our complicated, driven, and technologically distracted world, Anna can become our role model. We tend to neglect the wisdom of the older generation and look to the young for inspiration. But the Bible shines a light on the humble actions of an older woman, as I have done with Gladys and Ethel. Anna's story is included for a reason.

Some translations suggest that Anna was eighty-four; others that she was a widow for eighty-four years after being married for seven. If the latter is true, Luke's description of her being "very old" is fitting. Either way, she was a widow for a long time in an age when, despite the commandments, widows were often exploited or overlooked. Yet Anna, whose name means "grace," maintained her integrity, and trusted God to be her defense.

> **A father to the fatherless, a defender of widows, is God in his holy dwelling.**
>
> (Psalm 68:5)

Jesus and ...

My own mother was widowed at the age of forty-two. After the shock of losing her husband to cancer, she was left with a farm to run by herself and a family of four to raise on her own. A few years later, she also contracted cancer. As a young boy, I was unaware of the pain she felt during her debilitating treatment—she suffered silently and stoically. Like Anna, she was married for fewer years than she was widowed. The weight of widowhood is immense. In the first century, it must have been almost unbearable.

Yet throughout those long difficult years, Anna "never left the temple." We don't know whether she lived in the temple area, but she clearly never missed an opportunity to serve there. Interestingly, the Bible says that Anna and her father Penuel were "of the tribe of Asher," whose inheritance was northwest of Galilee, before they were exiled to Assyria (c.723 BC). So why was Anna living in Jerusalem? Perhaps she was a descendant of the faithful few who returned to the Lord in the time of King Hezekiah. Whatever her untold story, Anna was steadfast and faithful—and found her home in the temple.

At the king's command, couriers went throughout Israel and Judah with letters from the king and from his officials, which read: "People of Israel, return to the LORD, the God of Abraham, Isaac and Israel, that he may return to you who are left, who have escaped from the hand of the kings of Assyria. (2 Chronicles 30:6)

> **The couriers went from town to town in Ephraim and Manasseh, as far as Zebulun, but people scorned and ridiculed them. Nevertheless, some from Asher, Manasseh and Zebulun humbled themselves and went to Jerusalem.** (2 Chronicles 30:10-11)

Anna was not only perceptive, gracious, and faithful, she was also devout. Luke wrote that she "worshipped night and day, fasting and praying." Behind this simple statement are the hidden qualities of spirituality, self-denial, and longsuffering. She had a zeal for God's house—a characteristic she shared with both King David and her Messiah. These are qualities to which we can all aspire.

His disciples remembered that it is written: "Zeal for your house will consume me." (John 2:17)

Never be lacking in zeal, but keep your spiritual fervor, serving the Lord. Be joyful in hope, patient in affliction, faithful in prayer. (Romans 12:11-12)

Unhistoric acts

All great stories contain the sub-plots of minor characters who take the story forward and give insight into the main character. Anna is no exception. Her sub-plot has been incorporated into the greatest story in the world. After describing her life in just two verses, the Bible records her response to Jesus Christ in just one. It's such a simple verse that it is easy to ignore it, and yet it contains a wealth of wisdom.

> Coming up to them at that very moment, she gave thanks to God and spoke about the child to all who were looking forward to the redemption of Jerusalem.
> (Luke 2:38)

Most people in the temple that day wouldn't have noticed Anna's response, but Mary remembered it. Years later, Mary was almost certainly one of the sources for Luke's gospel and must have told him about their encounter. Luke clearly felt Anna's simple actions were significant enough to record for us.

All great stories contain the sub-plots of minor characters who take the story forward and give insight into the main character.

Jesus and ...

I spent much of my childhood in England witnessing similarly ordinary actions. Every day, on our family farm, Ted, our dairyman, would bring the cows in for milking. Whatever the weather or the season, his routines were the same. Our livelihood depended on it. And every year, in the fog-bound months of autumn, Philip, our plowman, would set out early to prepare the soil for the coming year. Again, our future depended on it. Few observed or praised their actions, but our fortunes relied on their resolute commitment and silent faithfulness.

> **The growing good of the world is partly dependent on unhistoric acts; and that things are not so ill with you and me as they might have been, is half owing to the number who lived faithfully a hidden life, and rest in unvisited tombs.**[7]
>
> (George Elliot)

What can we learn from Anna's seemingly unhistoric acts? First, she approached Mary, Joseph, and their child. The Bible uses the phrase "coming up to them." Despite the fact that they were complete strangers, she crossed the temple floor to talk to them. If you and I were in her position, would we have done the same? Or would we have used our uncertainty or insecurity as an excuse?

Of course, it was the recognition of Jesus Christ that caught her attention and drew her toward Him. But are we as determined as she was to build a relationship with Jesus? Anna's perception and resolve are exemplary. She put all else aside to gain one encounter with her Messiah—and such hunger and thirst are always rewarded. Perhaps Mary recognized something in the humility and passion of this older woman that she also possessed.

And Mary said: "My soul glorifies the Lord, and my spirit rejoices in God my Savior, for he has been mindful of the humble state of his servant. From now on all generations will call me blessed." (Luke 1:46–48)

He has filled the hungry with good things but has sent the rich away empty. (Luke 1:53)

But there is something else here that is also vital in the forging of relationships. Anna took the initiative. She didn't wait for something to happen or her witness to be confirmed. She took the first step. She took a risk and crossed the room. So many of us wait for others to approach us before we approach them. We want to be seen first. We want others to apologize first. Yet whether we are the sinner (which we all are) or the one sinned against (which we all are), the Bible encourages us to be the first to act. Anna's courage gives us a clue as to how to live a reconciled life.

> **Therefore, if you are offering your gift at the altar and there remember that your brother or sister has something against you, leave your gift there in front of the altar. First go and be reconciled to them; then come and offer your gift.** (Matthew 5:23-24)
>
> **If your brother or sister sins, go and point out their fault, just between the two of you. If they listen to you, you have won them over.** (Matthew 18:15)

But there is a second lesson we can draw from Anna's actions. The Bible says she approached the family "at that very moment," or more literally, "at that very hour." We don't know whether this means that she saw Simeon approach them first and was inspired by his response, or whether she simply waited for a pause in the presentation of their offerings. But whatever the exact moment, she saw an opportunity and she took it.

Some of my greatest regrets in life are not my foolish actions (of which there are many), but my missed opportunities. The moment I failed to pray for a woman—because I was too scared. The moment I failed to help a needy man—because it was inconvenient. The moment I failed to stop to assist someone at the side of the road—because I was in a hurry. These memories still haunt me to this day. I had a God-given opportunity to make a difference and I failed to act. But Anna's brief encounter in the temple is recorded for eternity. She had an hour and she filled it with significance.

Anna

The shadow of my finger cast
divides the future from the past;
Before it stands the unborn hour in
darkness and beyond thy power;
Behind its unreturning line the
vanished hour, no longer thine;
One hour alone is in thy hands, the
now on which the shadow stands.ª

(Written on a sundial)

Jesus and ...

> Gratitude was her posture and her lifestyle. For Anna, thanksgiving was the will of God—as it should be for us.

Another exemplary attribute is found in Anna's first reaction to seeing Jesus. The Bible says, "She gave thanks to God." Her thanksgiving was not dependent on her personal circumstances, but on her revelation of God. She entered the gates of the temple with thanksgiving, as the psalmist had encouraged, and then her unveiled eyes saw her Redeemer—and her heart overflowed with gratitude.

Many of us wait for something good to happen to us before we are grateful. Even then, our gratitude is often muted. But Anna didn't wait for her redemption to be realized, her prayers to be answered, or the will of God to be fulfilled in her life. Gratitude was her posture and her lifestyle. For Anna, thanksgiving was the will of God—as it should be for us.

Rejoice always, pray continually, give thanks in all circumstances; for this is God's will for you in Christ Jesus. (1 Thessalonians 5:16-18)

The fourth and final lesson we can learn from Anna's response in the temple is that her confession matched her revelation. Once she had seen Jesus, she spoke about Him. No doubt some of her audience were unimpressed. After all, she only had a brief encounter with a child in His mother's arms. But it seems she would not be silenced. She had caught a glimpse of our redemption—and she was compelled to share it.

Give thanks to the LORD, for he is good; his love endures forever. Let the redeemed of the LORD tell their story— those he redeemed from the hand of the foe.
(Psalm 107:1–2)

Anna's story is no less potent for its brevity. Although her story is reduced to a few short verses, they give us a glimpse of her ordinary, and yet extraordinary, qualities that are so prized by God—her courage, insight, and gratitude. Mary remembered them, Luke recorded them, and we should live them.

Jesus and ...

The way we live the mundane will often determine how we experience the miraculous.

Jesus and us

Like Anna's, much of our life is commonplace. It is often filled with everyday challenges, simple tasks, and daily routines. Yet it is these seemingly prosaic events, and the way we face them, that can enable us to live a life of significance. Most of Jesus' life, for instance, was shrouded in anonymity, and a great deal of His public life was ordinary. He ate with His friends, drank when He traveled, and slept where He could. He spent time walking, fishing, and even cooking. Yet these mundane activities were interspersed with His miracles. The way we live the mundane will often determine how we experience the miraculous.

The ordinary actions of Gladys and Ethel changed my life for the better and pointed me to Jesus Christ. Theirs was a life of significance and their story is worth telling. The ordinary actions of Anna were considered significant enough to be included in Scripture. She also points us to Jesus. Jesus and Anna is a story worth telling.

"Jesus and you" is also a story worth telling.

Jesus and ...

QUESTIONS TO CONSIDER

1. Anna's story was filled with ordinary routines and yet was valued enough to be included in the Scriptures (Luke 2:36-37). In what ways have you downplayed the mundane in your life?

2. Anna found significance in the ordinary routines of her daily life (Luke 2:36-38). In what ways can you encourage your friends and family to do the same?

3. Mary almost certainly told Anna's story to Luke (Luke 1:1-4), and I have told Gladys and Ethel's story to you. Who has had a similar impact on your life, and what did they teach you?

4. Anna had an encounter with Jesus during her daily devotional life (Luke 2:36-38). What can you learn from the regular devotions of the early church (Acts 2:42-47; Acts 13:1-3)?

5. Anna's prophetic insight (Luke 2:36-38) and Simeon's prophecy (Luke 2:25-35) encouraged Mary and Joseph. In what ways have prophecies impacted you?

6. Anna was a respected older person (Luke 2:36-38). How can we value older people better, and learn from their wisdom?

7. Anna is given prominence in the story of Jesus (Luke 2:36-38). What can we learn from Luke's portrayal of women in his gospel? (Luke 4:38-39; Luke 7:36-50; Luke 8:1-3; Luke 10:38-42; Luke 13:10-17)

8. Anna was not distracted when Jesus entered the temple (Luke 2:38). In which circumstances do you become distracted (Luke 10:38-41)? What have you learned from the missed opportunities in your life (John 20:24)?

9. Anna exemplified a life of worship and gratitude (Luke 2:36-38). In what ways can you foster greater gratitude in your life?

10. What has been your main takeaway from this chapter? What lessons have you learned that you can apply to your life today?

It has often been said that the two most important dates in our lives are the date we were born and the date we discover why.

77

Chapter Three

JESUS AND JOHN THE BAPTIST

Finding purpose in life

&

Jesus and ...

Several years ago, in Australia, I was talking to a group of people at the end of a church service in which I had just preached.

Suddenly a young man approached me, grabbed me by the lapels of my jacket and shouted, "What am I meant to do with my life?" As you can imagine, I was taken aback. I didn't know the man or his story, and yet there was no denying his passion or his desperation for an answer.

It has often been said that the two most important dates in our lives are the date we were born and the date we discover why. This young man knew the first date but not the second. He wanted to know why he was on this earth. He was desperate to discover his life purpose, his God-given destiny.

John the Baptist

> We all want to make a difference and to leave a mark and a legacy. We all want and need to know what we are fashioned for, what we are destined to be.

This search for purpose is not the sole domain of the desperate or the curious: it is common to humanity. We all want to make a difference and to leave a mark and a legacy. We all want and need to know what we are fashioned for, what we are destined to be. We may not share this young man's desperation—but we should share his desire.

Jesus and ...

Over the years, different authors have attempted to describe our search for purpose and the feeling of wellbeing we have when we discover it. This sense of meaning and satisfaction has been variously described as finding our "element,"[9] operating within our "flow,"[10] or more commonly, being in our "zone." But all of these writers are addressing a pursuit that is common to us all, and each of them conclude that if we discover our purpose, we will not only be more fulfilled but also more successful. However, I believe it is not just purpose we are searching for—but divine purpose. The Bible calls it a "calling."

There is something profoundly attractive about a person who knows what they do and why they do it. When I first met Colton Wickramaratne, to whom I referred earlier in this book, I was surprised by the authority with which he spoke. However, he was simply embodying his destiny. He knew that he was a prophet and spoke and behaved accordingly.

Similarly, when I first met the German evangelist Reinhard Bonnke, I was amazed at his focus and certainty. But he also knew why he had been born, and everything in his life was geared to that aim. Both these men had different gifts and yet both had found their specific purpose in life. They had both discovered their calling.

A minister who is sure of his call is among the most poised, confident, joy-filled, and effective of human beings; a minister who is not is among the most faltering and pitiable.[11] (Joel Nederhood)

Another person who discovered and embodied his calling was James Hudson Taylor. In 1849, as a young man, Taylor had an encounter with God in which he believed God called him to go to China. This became his life work. Within years he had set up the China Inland Mission, and his passion, conviction, and ministry impacted thousands of lives—including mine. His exemplary focus and eternal legacy were birthed at the moment of his divine calling.

> **From that hour his mind was made up. His pursuits and studies were all engaged in with reference to this object, and whatever difficulties presented themselves his purpose never wavered.**[12] (Amelia Taylor)

There are numerous examples of people throughout the Bible whose lives were transformed in the same way. For example, on the Damascus Road, Paul the apostle had an encounter with God that marked him for the rest of his life. His experience reveals that there are two aspects to a divine calling.

First, he was called to be set apart to God—to live a holy life. This was his general calling, one which all believers in Christ share. Second, he was called to fulfill a specific assignment—to be an apostle to the Gentiles. This was his specific calling, one which all believers in Christ should find out for themselves. It was this specific calling that the young man in Australia was so desperate to discover.

John the Baptist

About noon as I came near Damascus, suddenly a bright light from heaven flashed around me. I fell to the ground and heard a voice say to me, "Saul! Saul! Why do you persecute me?" "Who are you, Lord?" I asked.
"I am Jesus of Nazareth, whom you are persecuting," he replied. My companions saw the light, but they did not understand the voice of him who was speaking to me. "What shall I do, Lord?" I asked. "Get up," the Lord said, "and go into Damascus. There you will be told all that you have been assigned to do."
(Acts 22:6-10)

Although Paul has a great deal to teach us about the discovery and fulfillment of divine purpose, there is another person highlighted in the Gospels who I believe also personifies a called life—John the Baptist. Anyone who encountered John would have been in no doubt as to his mission and message. But what exactly were they? How did he discover them? How can John help you and me to find our purpose in life? That's what I intend to find out.

Jesus and ...

John's calling

In the fifteenth year of the reign of Tiberius Caesar—when Pontius Pilate was governor of Judea, Herod tetrarch of Galilee, his brother Philip tetrarch of Iturea and Traconitis, and Lysanias tetrarch of Abilene—during the high-priesthood of Annas and Caiaphas, the word of God came to John son of Zechariah in the wilderness. (Luke 3:1–2)

Luke's explanation of John's calling is carefully written. He describes a specific time, a significant place, and a particular person to whom "the word of God came." God clearly had a divine purpose to fulfill and so took the initiative to choose a person through whom He could fulfill it, and to whom He could give an assigned task. God's methodology, as we have noted, is people.

This pattern is found throughout the Bible. Isaiah the prophet was called at a specific time in history, the year of King Uzziah's death (see Isaiah 6:1–8). Moses was called in a significant place, near the mountain of God (see Exodus 3:1–10). And Esther was chosen to fulfill a particular task, the liberation of the Jewish people. Each of these servants of God discovered the confidence of calling. They knew that they were the right person, in the right place, at the right time. But with this God-given confidence came a divine responsibility.

> For if you remain silent at this time, relief and deliverance for the Jews will arise from another place, but you and your father's family will perish. And who knows but that you have come to your royal position for such a time as this.
> (Esther 4:14)

In each case, as with the calling of John the Baptist, God took the initiative and set the task. Neither Moses nor Isaiah nor Esther seemed to have had much of a choice in the matter of their calling. Their requirement was simply to say "yes." In an age where you and I are encouraged to make our own choices, and discover our own destiny, this kind of submission is countercultural, and yet it is the pathway to true freedom.

When I became a Christian in 1974, God called me to be a preacher, but I didn't want to be one; I wanted to be a biologist. So I said, "no." I rebelled against God and the task He had set for me, and like Jonah the prophet, I ran away. But God, in His merciful pursuit of my wellbeing, found me in a biology classroom three years later, and repeated His calling. He said, "You should be telling them about Me." This time, I said "yes." My somewhat reluctant but submissive response has defined my life ever since. It has proved to be one of the best decisions that I have ever made.

Of course, there is nothing wrong with being a biologist. It is an honorable profession. It could be your God-given calling. However, it wasn't what God wanted me to do. It wasn't my assigned task. My independent desire to do what I wanted wouldn't have attracted God's favor, but my dependent commitment to what He wanted guaranteed His fruit. God's assigned task for you may not be what you had planned or even wanted, but submission to God's calling is the most intelligent decision you can make.

We engage in evangelism today not because we want to, or because we choose to, or because we like to, but because we have been told to. We are under orders. We have no choice.[13] (Billy Graham)

I doubt that John the Baptist had always wanted to be a prophet, and I am sure that he wouldn't have chosen his troubled life or his traumatic death. Yet he has gone down in history as one of the greatest of men. He has been described as the last of the Old Testament prophets and the first of the New. He was a transitional leader, with all the challenges that transitions attract. He was a mediator between two testaments, an echo of the past and an emissary for the future. After four hundred years of silence, God chose to speak through this extraordinary messenger,

> He was a transitional leader, with all the challenges that transitions attract.

at a particular time in history. He was the right person, in the right place, at the right time.

Truly I tell you, among those born of women there has not risen anyone greater than John the Baptist; yet whoever is least in the kingdom of heaven is greater than he. (Matthew 11:11)

God has designed a world of transitions, a world of days and seasons. These transitions are reflected in the growth of every insect and revealed in the trunk of every tree. Transition is embedded into the very fabric of the natural world, and with every transition there is a resultant loss and gain, a decay and a renewal. The loss of leaves provides a seedbed for the future. The weeping of sowing is followed by the laughter of harvest.

> **As long as the earth endures, seedtime and harvest, cold and heat, summer and winter, day and night will never cease.**
> (Genesis 8:22)

Each of these natural transitions reveal a divine certainty and a human responsibility. The seasons are inevitable, but we must negotiate them successfully. As we each pass through the stages of life, or take another step on our pilgrimage, it is our ability to embrace the losses and transformation of these transitions that will determine our fruitfulness in life. That is why the study of a transitional leader such as John the Baptist can be so helpful. If he can do it, so can we. But what exactly was the task he was assigned? What was the message he was given, and how does it relate to our purpose in life?

John's Message

The influential German preacher Balthasar Hubmaier (1480–1528) was a reformer and an anabaptist, and he lived in a turbulent time in history. Europe was in transition. The old order was being challenged and changed, and new ideas and beliefs were coming to the fore. The Protestant Reformation was beginning to transform the world.

In this tumultuous season, Hubmaier found certainty and guidance in the life of John the Baptist and based his ministry on the three aspects of John's message: preaching, baptism, and pointing people to Jesus Christ. These trademarks became Hubmaier's calling and purpose. Let's look at the first of these marks of John's preaching in more detail.

John said to the crowds coming out to be baptized by him, "You brood of vipers! Who warned you to flee from the coming wrath? Produce fruit in keeping with repentance. And do not begin to say to yourselves, 'We have Abraham as our father.' For I tell you that out of these stones God can raise up children for Abraham. The ax is already at the root of the trees, and every tree that does not produce good fruit will be cut down and thrown into the fire." "What should we do then?" the crowd asked. John answered, "Anyone who has two shirts should share with the one who has none, and anyone who has food should do the same." Even tax collectors came to be baptized. "Teacher," they asked, "what should we do?" "Don't collect any more than you are required to," he told them. Then some soldiers asked him, "And what should we do?" He replied, "Don't extort money and don't accuse people falsely— be content with your pay."

(Luke 3:7–14)

Jesus and ...

I suspect that many of us in today's ultra-sensitive world would find John's preaching hard to take. If I started my message by calling my listeners a "brood of vipers," I would be castigated on social media. But what exactly was John doing? He was preaching a message of repentance that demanded a change of heart and mind, and also allowed for no excuses. There is no doubt it was a challenging message, but it was what the times demanded.

What was the response to John's timely message? His audience, which Luke says consisted of the common people, tax collectors, and soldiers, were all cut to the heart, and each of them responded in the same way: "What should we do?"

The world in which we live is stained with tragedy. Every time we look at the news, we are reminded of political crises and global conflicts. Economic, environmental, and epidemiological disasters haunt our minds. Young people face a future of uncertainties and anxieties. It seems as if the world is in a state of flux—a season of transition. So maybe John's message is exactly what we need to hear. And perhaps his crowd's reaction is exactly how we need to respond.

The English theologian Tom Wright suggested that the best response to the Covid-19 pandemic was not "Why is this happening?" but rather "What can we do?"

> Sorrow rises from the world like a pall of smoke, shaping the question we hardly dare ask: Why? Actually, the best answer I've heard in the last few weeks has not been to the question "Why?" It's been to the question "What?" What can we do?[14]
>
> (Tom Wright)

The second characteristic of John's message was baptism. The word *baptism* refers to transformation through immersion, as in a cloth immersed in dye, or an onion immersed in vinegar. All "baptisms," and there are several mentioned in the Bible, involve a cutting off from the past, a necessary and often difficult transition, and a commitment to a new future. John's baptism was a baptism in water, a baptism of repentance, but he also prophesied another baptism—an immersion with the Holy Spirit.

Jesus and ...

John answered them all, "I baptize you with water. But one who is more powerful than I will come, the straps of whose sandals I am not worthy to untie. He will baptize you with the Holy Spirit and fire. His winnowing fork is in his hand to clear his threshing floor and to gather the wheat into his barn, but he will burn up the chaff with unquenchable fire." (Luke 3:16–17)

The baptism in the Spirit, which John prophesied and which was fulfilled at Pentecost, was the beginning of a new era—the birth of the church. The disciples needed to be empowered for their divine purpose—to be witnesses for Jesus Christ. Only an immersion in the Spirit would be able to transform this small group of ineffective men and women and empower them with the courage to change the world. It's a baptism we all need.

> On one occasion, while he was eating with them, he gave them this command: "Do not leave Jerusalem, but wait for the gift my Father promised, which you have heard me speak about. For John baptized with water, but in a few days you will be baptized with the Holy Spirit."
> (Acts 1:4–5)

However, John's prophecy also included a baptism of fire. He used the image of a threshing floor, an image that is common throughout the Bible. Threshing floors were places of fellowship and fruitfulness, sacrifice and separation. They were places where the community gathered to separate the wheat from the chaff. It is not coincidental that the temple was built on a threshing floor. The English word *tribulation* comes from the Latin word *tribulum*, the spiked board used for threshing wheat. John's message is both a call to power and a call to purity. Both John and Hubmaier knew that times of transition and tribulation need both.

Then Solomon began to build the temple of the Lord in Jerusalem on Mount Moriah, where the Lord had appeared to his father David. It was on the threshing floor of Araunah the Jebusite, the place provided by David. (2 Chronicles 3:1)

The final and overarching characteristic of John the Baptist's message was his passion to point people to Jesus Christ. This passion overrode his own desires. In order to proclaim the good news, Christ had to be exalted while he had to be humbled. He decided to highlight Christ and allow himself to slip into the shadows. When he pointed to Christ, he pointed away from himself, and his followers left him to follow the Lamb of God. It's one of the immensely attractive attributes of John, and one that is essential in a time of uncertainty and self-centeredness.

The next day John was there again with two of his disciples. When he saw Jesus passing by, he said, "Look, the Lamb of God!" When the two disciples heard him say this, they followed Jesus.

(John 1:35-37)

> Each step is vital: repentance, baptism, and submission to Christ; a change of mind, a change of priorities, and a change of Lord.

These three ingredients in John's message are the first steps toward the discovery of our purpose. Each step is vital: repentance, baptism, and submission to Christ; a change of mind, a change of priorities, and a change of Lord. If we follow his example, as Hubmaier did, we will begin to find ourselves living a life of significance. But John didn't just preach this message, he lived it.

John's Identity

The incarnation of Christ is not only a profound mystery, but also a divine pattern. The messengers of Christ need to embody the message they bring and personify the purpose they fulfill. John the Baptist certainly exemplified this principle. The man himself was his sermon. Everything about his life and lifestyle pointed to Jesus. He became the prophecy that was spoken about him. He was not only the fulfillment of a prophecy; he was a prophecy.

> He went into all the country around the Jordan, preaching a baptism of repentance for the forgiveness of sins. As it is written in the book of the words of Isaiah the prophet: "A voice of one calling in the wilderness, 'Prepare the way for the Lord, make straight paths for him. Every valley shall be filled in, every mountain and hill made low. The crooked roads shall become straight, the rough ways smooth. And all people will see God's salvation.'" (Luke 3:3-6)

In the same way that Isaiah became a sign, as I have already noted, John symbolized the prophetic purpose for which he was sent. There is something profoundly validating to know that we are a fulfillment of prophecy and an answer to prayer. This, I believe, is an important part of our discovery of purpose.

Although I cannot begin to compare myself with John, I have attempted, like Hubmaier, to model myself on his ministry. So, when a prophet prophesied over me and said, "You're a teacher, teacher, teacher, teacher, teacher. That's what you are. Everything about you is a teacher," it was an encouraging endorsement of my calling. This prophet didn't just speak about what I was doing, he spoke about who I am—who God has called me to be.

However, John wasn't just a prophecy—he was also a voice for God. He didn't share his own opinions, as so many of us do, nor did he speak "his own truth," as is so often encouraged in today's world. He was a witness to *the* Truth. He spoke the very words of God and so became a forerunner of the One who only spoke God's words. This is the key to fruitful ministry.

For I did not speak on my own, but the Father who sent me commanded me to say all that I have spoken. I know that his command leads to eternal life. So whatever I say is just what the Father has told me to say. (John 12:49-50)

John's voice confronted the voices of his day. Both his life and his sermons were challenging. He lived in the wilderness, beyond the Jordan, and preached with some of its harsh characteristics. He was an outsider with a difficult message and an uncomfortable manner. He didn't try to fit in or be accepted. His entire demeanor challenged the status quo. He sought to influence the world from the edges. People who don't attempt to conform to the world's expectations and who are also comfortable in their own skin, are much more likely to find God's will for their life.

> **Do not conform to the pattern of this world, but be transformed by the renewing of your mind. Then you will be able to test and approve what God's will is—his good, pleasing and perfect will.**
> (Romans 12:2)

There is one more attribute of John's identity, which is worth considering here. He was not only a voice, a prophecy, and an outsider—he was also a way-maker. He made a way for Jesus; he straightened the path toward salvation. This was part of John's specific calling, his assigned task—but is it one that we can emulate?

Paul the apostle gives us a clue. He encouraged his disciple Timothy to handle the word of God properly. The original Greek word he used (*orthotomeo*) means "to cut a straight path," as a plowman might cut a furrow or a road-maker may cut a swathe across the landscape. By studying the word of God correctly, as Paul encouraged Timothy to do, we will not just make a way for Jesus, as John did, we will make a way for others and ourselves.

> **Do your best to present yourself to God as one approved, a worker who does not need to be ashamed and who correctly handles the word of truth.**
> (2 Timothy 2:15)

John's example

John the Baptist's life and message not only give us a clue as to how we can live for God in a world in crisis, but also how we can discover our life purpose. John was transformed by the message he preached, found his identity in his relationship with

Jesus Christ, and lived a life of significance because of the call he received. He exemplified what every one of us is looking for in life: transformation, connection, and significance. These three ideas are keys to unlocking a life of fulfillment and destiny.

First, we need to be transformed. As we have seen, God has designed a world of change. Even though all of us find change difficult, transformation and growth are hard-wired into our physiology and our psyche. But if only our bodies and brains change, we won't reach our full potential as human beings. We need to change spiritually. This is where John's message is so helpful.

We need to repent, be baptized, and allow Jesus Christ to transform us from the inside out. Even though John's baptism was only a foretaste of what was to come, it was a signpost toward the spiritual transformation we all need.

Peter replied, "Repent and be baptized, every one of you, in the name of Jesus Christ for the forgiveness of your sins. And you will receive the gift of the Holy Spirit. The promise is for you and your children and for all who are far off—for all whom the Lord our God will call." (Acts 2:38–39)

Second, we need connection. John the Baptist is inextricably linked to Jesus Christ. We cannot think of him without reference to his Messiah. His identity was established by the words spoken about

He found his identity in God's Son and God's words. John is eternally connected to Jesus—as we should be.

him by the prophet Isaiah, and also his relationship with Jesus. Unsurprisingly, he is known as "the Baptist." In a world where we are encouraged to identify ourselves, John's example stands out. He didn't define himself, he was defined by God and God only. He found his identity in God's Son and God's words. John is eternally connected to Jesus—as we should be.

This is a critical message for our independent and uncertain times. In the equally troubled and transitional times of the early church, Paul the apostle was at pains to point out that we discover who we are in Christ. Like a hermit crab finds its home and protection in the shell of another, our security, purpose, and hope are found in Him.

In him we were also chosen, having been predestined according to the plan of him who works out everything in conformity with the purpose of his will, in order that we, who were the first to put our hope in Christ, might be for the praise of his glory. (Ephesians 1:11–12)

Third, we need significance in our lives. Once John the Baptist was transformed and identified, he began to live a life of purpose. This is a pattern that we can all follow. When we have been transformed by Christ, and eternally connected with Him, we are in a position to live our general calling and discover our specific task. Ultimately, our purpose in life is not about what we want, but about what God wants for us. It is not about our strengths,

Jesus and ...

but about His strength in us. It's not about our destiny, but about His glory. This is how John lived.

This pathway to purpose may seem alien to us, but it is the way to true fulfillment. After I gave my life to Jesus Christ, I needed to allow Him to change me from the inside out, until I was inextricably connected to Him, and until I was ready to say "yes" to His specific calling for my life—to be a teacher of God's Word. Although initially I didn't want to be a preacher, I have found an inexpressible joy in submitting to God's purpose for my life.

Once again, the steps on this path are change, connection, and calling; or as John the apostle describes it, message, fellowship, and joy. These are steps we can all follow.

> We proclaim to you what we have seen and heard, so that you also may have fellowship with us. And our fellowship is with the Father and with his Son, Jesus Christ. We write this to make our joy complete.
>
> (1 John 1:3–4)

Jesus and us

John the Baptist was devastated by the sin and hopelessness of the world in which he lived and longed for people to find hope in Jesus Christ. As a result, he can come across as an angry man. But in reality, as I have attempted to demonstrate, he was simply a man of deep passions and clear purpose. Nonetheless, his righteous anger can give us a final clue about the discovery of our specific calling.

When the young man grabbed me by the lapels and shouted, "What am I meant to do with my life," he expressed a desire that is common to all of us. He wanted to know his life's purpose. I could have told him to follow the example of John the Baptist, as I have with you. But instead I asked, "What makes you angry?"

I explained that I didn't mean his daily frustrations or his sinful responses, of which there were many. I was asking about a righteous indignation, a deeply held desire for justice, a God-given passion—an indicator of his assigned task.

After some thought, he replied, "I'll tell you what makes me angry—when men mistreat women." I said, "Well, now you know what to do with your life—go and change that."

So, what makes you angry?

Jesus and ...

QUESTIONS TO CONSIDER

1. John the Baptist lived, preached, and was called in the wilderness (Luke 1:80; Luke 3:1-4; Matthew 3:1-3). In what ways does his wilderness experience apply to us (Deuteronomy 8:2; Hosea 2:14; Luke 4:1)?

2. Balthasar Hubmaier modeled his ministry on the message of John the Baptist (Luke 3:1-4; John 1:29-37). Which biblical character do you relate to and what aspect of their life do you seek to emulate?

3. John the Baptist personified his calling (Luke 3:1-6). Who have you known who has embodied their calling and what have you learned from them?

4. John the Baptist was a transitional leader (Luke 3:15-18). In what ways do transitions require leadership (Joshua 1:1-2)?

5. The hearers of John the Baptist's message responded with the question, "What should we do?" (Luke 3:7-14). What does that phrase teach us about repentance?

John the Baptist

6. John the Baptist lived as an "outsider" and yet communicated to "insiders" (Mark 1:4-8). How can we communicate effectively to the world and yet not conform to its pattern (Romans 12:2; John 17:13-19)?

7. John the Baptist's ministry was to prepare the way for Jesus (Matthew 3:1-3). How can we do this successfully in our own world (2 Peter 3:3-13)?

8. John the Baptist knew his God-given purpose and lived accordingly (Mark 1:1-8). If you know your God-given calling, how has it changed your life? If you don't know your assigned task, how do you intend to discover it?

9. John the Baptist was zealous about his purpose and message (Luke 3:7-9). In what ways should zeal play a part in our lives (Psalm 69:9; John 2:17; Romans 12:11)?

10. What has been your main takeaway from this chapter? What lessons have you learned that you can apply to your life today?

We all want to be part of a community where we are loved and valued. We all want to be liked. This has been true throughout history.

107
Chapter Four

JESUS AND THE MAN WITH LEPROSY

Finding acceptance and healing

&

Jesus and ...

I was seven years old when I was sent to boarding school.

Even though it was an excellent school, and I was immensely privileged to attend, I couldn't shake off the profound sense of rejection that I felt when I was left there by my mother. This rejection became even more deeply entrenched when my father died a year later. It seemed as though I had been abandoned by both my parents. In my grief I sought affection and acceptance from others, only to be misunderstood by the teachers and bullied by my peers. I began to question my value until feelings of rejection and worthlessness became my constant companions.

Of course, my experience may be completely different to yours. You may have always known that you were loved and may never have known rejection. You may not have questioned your own worth. But whatever your story, I am sure you will have observed the devastation of abandonment and the power of acceptance. Every one of us seeks acknowledgment. We all want to be part of a community where we are loved and valued. We all want to be liked. This has been true throughout history.

The Man with Leprosy

The book of Luke is filled with these stories of abandonment and acceptance. However, on first reading, they seem so different from our own stories that we are tempted to pass them off as irrelevant. But as we read them more closely, we discover that they address problems that are common to humanity, and have been included in the gospel, not just as a record of some extraordinary events, but as a salve for our deepest needs. One of these is the story of a man with leprosy.

While Jesus was in one of the towns, a man came along who was covered with leprosy. When he saw Jesus, he fell with his face to the ground and begged him, "Lord, if you are willing, you can make me clean." Jesus reached out his hand and touched the man. "I am willing," he said. "Be clean!" And immediately the leprosy left him. (Luke 5:12-13)

Leprosy, or Hansen's disease as it is more commonly known today, still impacts about two hundred thousand people every year worldwide. It is a treatable bacterial infection that causes an inability to feel physical pain. As a result, injuries can go untreated and become infected, which occasionally leads to disfigurement. Over the years, this condition has been tragically misunderstood. People with leprosy have had a cruel history.

Jesus and ...

Leprosy sufferers have always been relegated to the edges of society. Humanity marginalizes those it fears or fails to understand. In many countries, up until the twentieth century, victims of leprosy were incarcerated in leper colonies or secluded in leprosariums. They became outcasts from society. The stigma and shame associated with such seclusion must have been indescribable. My boarding school experience pales into insignificance.

An inmate who had come in to mop the floor whispered to me. "That lady," he said, pointing toward the old lady (Ella), "she got the leprosy when she was twelve years old. Her daddy dropped her off one day and never came back." Then he asked, "Still feeling sorry for yourself?" I guessed the woman was close to eighty. That would mean she'd been here for about sixty-eight years.[15]
(Neil White)

In the Old Testament times, there were specific laws that prevented people with skin diseases, such as leprosy, from engaging with the community. They were considered unclean and were segregated from society. No one was immune from these laws. Even Uzziah, the King of Judah, was condemned to living separately and was excluded from the house of God for the rest of his life. The consequences of carrying this sickness were severe and lifelong, and every victim suffered in every part of their being—spirit, soul, and body.

The Man with Leprosy

Anyone with such a defiling disease must wear torn clothes, let their hair be unkempt, cover the lower part of their face and cry out, "Unclean! Unclean!" As long as they have the disease they remain unclean. They must live alone; they must live outside the camp.
(Leviticus 13:45–46)

The history of the disease makes Jesus' behavior toward those suffering from leprosy all the more remarkable. He approached the unapproachable, touched the untouchable, and accepted the unacceptable. But in the nation of Israel, where the laws were strict, and sickness was attributed to sinfulness, He also did the unimaginable. By healing leprosy, Jesus proclaimed a new kingdom, introduced a new covenant, and demonstrated that He was a new High Priest to whom the rejected could return and find cleansing, wholeness, and acceptance.

Jesus and ...

> As he was going into a village, ten men who had leprosy met him. They stood at a distance and called out in a loud voice, "Jesus, Master, have pity on us!" When he saw them, he said, "Go, show yourselves to the priests." And as they went, they were cleansed. One of them, when he saw he was healed, came back, praising God in a loud voice. He threw himself at Jesus' feet and thanked him—and he was a Samaritan. Jesus asked, "Were not all ten cleansed? Where are the other nine? Has no one returned to give praise to God except this foreigner?" Then he said to him, "Rise and go; your faith has made you well." (Luke 17:12–19)

Several years ago while visiting Pakistan, some friends and I were invited to speak to the nomads who lived in makeshift tents on the filthy rubbish dumps on the outskirts of the cities. They had been marginalized because of their conditions and excluded because of their customs. They were outsiders. When we entered one tent, where many of them had gathered to hear us speak, every eye was fixed on us. It was a confronting experience. I had never seen such desperate people.

Of course, I had no idea what to speak about. What did I know of their circumstances? What pain did we have in common? What hope could I bring? Despite these uncertainties, I began to tell them about the story of the leper who Jesus was willing to cleanse. They had never heard the story. They had never heard of Jesus. But as I described how a King had once walked this earth to bring good news to the poor, they all began to weep. They saw themselves in the story. They wanted to meet the One who had reached out to the leper—and to them.

Go back and report to John what you have seen and heard: The blind receive sight, the lame walk, those who have leprosy are cleansed, the deaf hear, the dead are raised, and the good news is proclaimed to the poor. (Luke 7:22)

Recipients of grace

I have never suffered from leprosy, or been secluded from society, or lived on a rubbish dump, but my experience in Pakistan taught me that I have much more in common with the marginalized than I initially thought. I was also an outsider, excluded from the blessings and benefits of a faith community. I have also heard the good news proclaimed to the poor. I have also been touched by God.

If we are going to learn from Jesus' encounters with people with leprosy, we first need to identify with their story. We need to remember that we were also outcasts, excluded from the wellbeing of belonging. We were also recipients of grace. But unlike the sentence of separation forced on those suffering from leprosy, we were unclean by choice. Our disease was internal, a leprosy of the mind—a dirtiness of soul. We needed the cleansing blood of Jesus. We still need it.

Jesus and ...

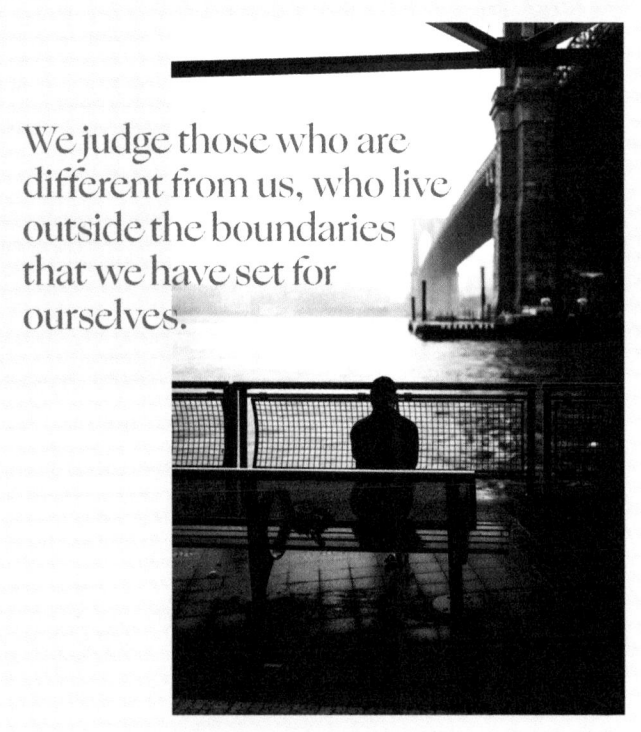

> We judge those who are different from us, who live outside the boundaries that we have set for ourselves.

Remember that at that time you were separate from Christ, excluded from citizenship in Israel and foreigners to the covenants of the promise, without hope and without God in the world. But now in Christ Jesus you who once were far away have been brought near by the blood of Christ. (Ephesians 2:12-13)

We live in a generation that makes much of strengths and thinks little of weaknesses. We tend to talk about our mistakes or failures and not about our sins. Yet in the kingdom of God, faith is preceded by repentance, and repentance is predicated on an acknowledgment of our sinfulness. We must never forget that we have been cleansed from our past sins. This remembrance is the foundation of our gratitude and the empowerment for our fruitfulness.

For this very reason, make every effort to add to your faith goodness; and to goodness, knowledge; and to knowledge, self-control; and to self-control, perseverance; and to perseverance, godliness; and to godliness, mutual affection; and to mutual affection, love. For if you possess these qualities in increasing measure, they will keep you from being ineffective and unproductive in your knowledge of our Lord Jesus Christ. But whoever does not have them is nearsighted and blind, forgetting that they have been cleansed from their past sins. (2 Peter 1:5–9)

If we fail to remember that we were desperately in need of cleansing, that we were also outsiders, we can become critical of the poor, the broken, and the marginalized. We judge those who live on the outskirts of the city, on the edges of society. We judge those who are different from us, who live outside the boundaries that we have set for ourselves. We judge the exile, the stranger, and the refugee. We judge because we have forgotten that we were also disfigured and powerless to change. We judge because we forget that we have been found—and included. How can I judge those living amid the refuse of a city simply because I was rescued first?

Jesus and ...

> **To be deprived of the use of one's limbs is little help to one in carrying out the work of government. If only I could be cured of the disease of Naaman, but I have found no Elisha to heal me.**[16]
>
> (King Baldwin IV, The Leper King)

The stories of suffering in Luke's gospel are a world away from comfortable Christianity. It's only as we remember that before the King found us, before we were included in Christ, before we found acceptance in the community of the church—we were unclean, powerless, and hopeless outcasts. But there is something else we need to remember, something else that we have in common with those suffering with leprosy. We can become unfeeling. In our case, a mental leprosy—a heartless inability to feel the pain of others. There is a word in the Greek New Testament (*astorgos*) that can be translated as "hardhearted, heartless, unfeeling, without natural affection—without love." It is a characteristic of the last days.

It's only as we remember that before the King found us, before we were included in Christ before we found acceptance in the community of the church—we were unclean, powerless, and hopeless outcasts.

> **But mark this: There will be terrible times in the last days. People will be lovers of themselves, lovers of money, boastful, proud, abusive, disobedient to their parents, ungrateful, unholy, without love, unforgiving, slanderous, without self-control, brutal, not lovers of the good, treacherous, rash, conceited, lovers of pleasure rather than lovers of God—having a form of godliness but denying its power. Have nothing to do with such people.** (2 Timothy 3:1-5)

The gospel that Luke so carefully investigated is not just a historical record about other people in another place, it is also about us in the here and now. It is our story. In the gospel, the excluded found belonging and acceptance in Christ—they discovered their sub-plot in God's story. As we identify with them, we can also receive hope for change. But we also need to understand what, exactly, Jesus did for those suffering from leprosy—and what it means for us today.

Reaching out

It's immensely difficult to place yourself in the shoes of others. Even if we have shared experiences, it doesn't mean we understand their pain or their joy. Only God knows our motives and our thoughts. Although I have lost my father, it doesn't follow that I can comprehend what it means for others to lose theirs. Everyone's suffering is unique. So even if we have had leprosy, we can't possibly know what it meant for the man with leprosy to be healed. However, we can ask ourselves what Jesus did for him and whether Jesus has done the same for us. We can also ask ourselves whether we have helped others in the same way.

> **Jesus reached out his hand and touched the man. "I am willing," he said. "Be clean!" And immediately the leprosy left him. Then Jesus ordered him, "Don't tell anyone, but go, show yourself to the priest and offer the sacrifices that Moses commanded for your cleansing, as a testimony to them."**
> (Luke 5:13–14)

By reaching out and touching the man with leprosy, Jesus placed value on a man whom few had valued before. This is an extraordinary truth that we can draw from this story. Jesus loved him, touched him, and spoke to him. This was the first and perhaps greatest step in the man's healing. To be seen in the crowd and to be noticed is one thing, but to be chosen and graced is quite another. To know that someone believes in us, sees potential in us, and wants the best for us is a priceless revelation. This is what Jesus Christ has done for each one of us.

Many years ago, I was speaking in a military Christian fellowship. The room was filled with smartly uniformed personnel. The other speakers included a general, a brigadier, and a lieutenant colonel. To be honest, I wondered why I was there. Nonetheless, I did my best to bring an encouraging and relevant message. At the end of the meeting, a man approached me from the back of the room. His appearance indicated that he was no longer a serving soldier, and his manner suggested that his service had been underappreciated. He simply said, "Thank you. Today, you have added value to my life." That's why I was there. That's why we are all here.

Therefore, as God's chosen people, holy and dearly loved, clothe yourselves with compassion, kindness, humility, gentleness and patience. Bear with each other and forgive one another if any of you has a grievance against someone. Forgive as the Lord forgave you. And over all these virtues put on love, which binds them all together in perfect unity. (Colossians 3:12-14)

Once we have been chosen and valued, as Jesus Christ did for the man with leprosy, it's our responsibility and privilege to reach out to others. The sacrifice and commitment of the Moravian church is a great example. When leper colonies were set up to seclude those suffering from the disease, members of the church would join their community in order to help them; knowing that they might not only catch the disease, but also may never be allowed to return to freedom.

In 1846, for instance, after Robben Island in Cape Town (where Nelson Mandela was later imprisoned) had been set up as a leper colony, Joseph and Friederike Lehmann moved there to continue their work. They had experienced the touch of Christ and now felt compelled to place value on others. Their compassion had a profound influence on the community.

According to one Moravian source the Lehmanns were welcomed as "the whole company of lepers broke forth in songs of praise to the Lord, who had restored to them their beloved father and mother."[17] (Moravian Church Archives)

Willing to identify

The willingness of the Moravians to reach out to, and identify with, the lepers on Robben Island seems almost shocking to our often comfortable suburban Christianity—but should it be so remarkable? The Moravians knew that they were former outcasts and recipients of grace, and so they purposely reached out to other outcasts in need of grace.

We don't know the response of the man with leprosy who was cleansed by Jesus. Jesus ordered him not to tell anyone about his healing until he had been pronounced clean by the priests, but what did he do after that? Did he return to a normal life in the community that had banished him? Or did he return to the other lepers with a powerful story and some good news? What would our response have been? What should our response be?

Jesus and ...

> Jesus knew that the power within Him was greater than any sickness. Once again, the good news is that this same power can dwell within us.

Of course, we all know that we should walk as Jesus walked, but it is often not as easy as that, is it? Nonetheless, when Jesus willingly and purposely reached out and touched the man with leprosy, He revealed two motivations from which we can draw inspiration.

First, Jesus was compelled by compassion. The root word used for "compassion" in the Greek New Testament is the one used for "bowels." Some, in fact, translate the word *compassion* as "bowels of mercy." It's a deeply felt, God-given longing for lost souls to be found, and the sick to be healed. This is what motivated Jesus to identify with the marginalized and reconcile the excluded to community. The good news is that this same compassion can also compel us.

For Christ's love compels us, because we are convinced that one died for all, and therefore all died. And he died for all, that those who live should no longer live for themselves but for him who died for them and was raised again. (2 Corinthians 5:14–15)

The second motivation that we can observe in this story is Jesus' intense desire to give something of Himself, to impart the power that He had to others. Where people in the community avoided lepers because they believed that they would catch the disease and become unclean, Jesus knew that the power within Him was greater than any sickness. Once again, the good news is that this same power can dwell within us.

When Jesus touched the leper, He became unclean in the eyes of the community. However, the theologian Scot McKnight argues that the purity of Jesus was more contagious than leprosy. In effect, Jesus infected the unclean man with His own purity. In doing so, He foreshadowed the great exchange, where He would become unclean to make us clean; where He would be rejected so that we could be accepted; where He identified with us so that we could identify with Him.

Everyone in Judaism knows that impurity is contagious. It spreads to whatever touches it. That is why humans are classified and segregated into the pure and impure. In contrast, purity is not contagious. Until Jesus comes. Jesus is the first contagion of purity. Jesus lives for us, and he becomes impure for us so that he can touch us and "infect" us with his purity.[18]
(Scot McKnight)

So, what does it mean to identify with Jesus Christ—to follow Him? Jesus purposely sought out the marginalized. He willingly identified with the unclean. During His life He ate with the despised, and at His death He suffered among the rejected—outside the community. What will compel us to go to the edges of society as He did? What gift do we need?

> The high priest carries the blood of animals into the Most Holy Place as a sin offering, but the bodies are burned outside the camp. And so Jesus also suffered outside the city gate to make the people holy through his own blood. Let us, then, go to him outside the camp, bearing the disgrace he bore.
>
> (Hebrews 13:11-13)

The gift of pain

So far, we have noted that the man with leprosy was valued, cleansed, and restored to community—as we have been. But there is one more observation that we can draw from this story. An implication that is often overlooked. When Jesus healed this man and the leprosy left him, his pain returned.

For months, perhaps years, the man had slowly lost feeling in his limbs, until he could no longer feel pain. His diseased hands became infected, and he couldn't reach out to touch others as he had done before. But now he was healed—and hurting. But for him, the pain wasn't a sign of a sickness—it was a sign of his restored humanity ... it was a gift.

In 1946, while working in a leprosy sanatorium, the physician Paul Brand discovered that the deformities of leprosy were not an intrinsic part of the disease, but rather a consequence of the progressive devastation of infection and injury, which occurred because the patient was unable to feel pain. In 1972, he wrote: "If I had one gift which I could give to people with leprosy, it would be the gift of pain."[19] (Stephen Grosz)

When we become followers of Christ, we are restored to our true selves. We discover our true humanity as we worship in gratitude at the feet of Jesus. But our salvation is not selfish. Our forgiveness enables us to forgive others, our healing carries a responsibility for others, and our comfort is given to be shared. With the gift of life, we are also given the gift of pain. We begin to understand suffering in a way that we have never understood it before. Our pain enables us to feel the pain of others—it is the gift we need in order to reach out and touch others. However, it is not our pain that we share with the world; it is God's comfort. It is not our pain that qualifies us to help others; it is the grace that we have received.

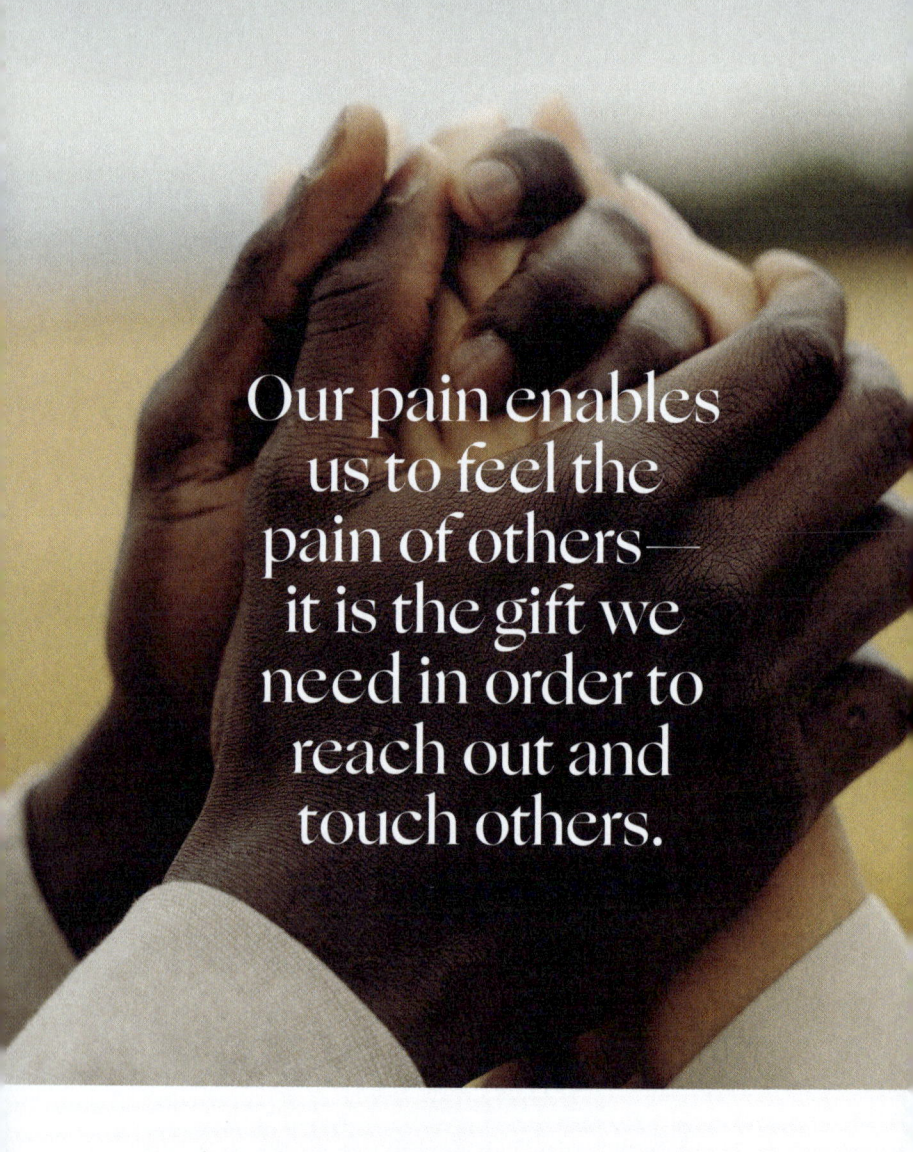

> Our pain enables us to feel the pain of others—it is the gift we need in order to reach out and touch others.

Praise be to the God and Father of our Lord Jesus Christ, the Father of compassion and the God of all comfort, who comforts us in all our troubles, so that we can comfort those in any trouble with the comfort we ourselves receive from God. (2 Corinthians 1:3-4)

Jesus and us

In the 1990s, Neil White was incarcerated for kiting, in a minimum security prison in Louisiana. The prison at Carville, he discovered, was also a leprosarium. In his book, *A Sanctuary of Outcasts*, he describes how he was deeply impacted by the faith and dignity of those suffering from leprosy. On his release, he determined to find a church that was similar to the one at Carville—a place where the broken could find help, forgiveness, and acceptance.

> **I didn't know if a church like this existed, but if it did I would go. And I would pray. Not the kind of prayers I used to say for miracles or money or advancement. I would ask for something more simple. I would pray for recollection—pray that I would never forget.**[20] (Neil White)

The phrase "a sanctuary of outcasts" is a wonderful description of the church. A place where recipients of grace find cleansing and wholeness. A place of worship and gratitude. A place of remembrance and reaching out to others. A church reminiscent of Jesus' parable of the net (see Matthew 13:47–50), which is filled with all kinds of fish, and where Jesus alone judges between the insiders and the outsiders.

Could we create a community like that?

Jesus and ...

QUESTIONS TO CONSIDER

1. The man with leprosy was excluded from his community (Leviticus 13:45-46; Luke 5:12-16). Have you been rejected by other people? How did it make you feel?

2. People with leprosy were unable to enter the temple (Leviticus 13:45-46; Luke 5:12-16). From what were they excluded and what can we learn from their experience (Ephesians 2:11-13)?

3. Jesus purposely reached out to excluded people (Luke 17:11-19; John 4:4-42). Who are some examples of rejected people in your world? In what ways can you reach out to them?

4. Jesus was willing to heal the man with leprosy (Luke 5:12-13). What can this story teach us about the will of God in our lives (Matthew 6:9-10)?

5. Jesus cleansed ten lepers, but only one Samaritan returned to give thanks (Luke 17:11-19). Why did Jesus draw attention to this "foreigner"? What can we learn from his example (2 Peter 1:9; Luke 7:47)?

6. One of the characteristics of "the last days" is that people will become unfeeling, heartless, "without love" (2 Timothy 3:1-5). In what ways have you observed this to be true in your own world?

7. Jesus told the cleansed lepers to show themselves to the priests (Luke 5:14; Luke 17:14). What was the significance of this and what is a modern equivalent?

8. Members of the Moravian church exemplified extraordinary compassion toward those suffering from leprosy. Who has inspired you with a similar act of compassion? How can you follow their example?

9. Jesus taught that the kingdom of God was like a net that contains "all kind of fish" (Matthew 13:47-50). What steps do we need to take to help our churches become sanctuaries for outcasts?

10. What has been your main takeaway from this chapter? What lessons have you learned that you can apply to your life today?

We all make judgments. It is part of our human nature—part of our sinfulness.

Chapter Five

JESUS AND THE CENTURION

Finding faith in a time of unbelief

&

Jesus and ...

In the 1970s, I went to a Chinese restaurant with two friends. It was in a very run-down neighborhood, and as it was around midnight, we were the only customers.

We pooled all our cash and we had just enough for the set meal. But when we finished, the owner overcharged us and we couldn't pay. We started arguing. We thought we had been conned and the owner thought he had been cheated. Eventually, he locked the door of the restaurant, got out a knife, and demanded payment. It was a tense moment. But the problem was not about money, it was about judgment. Each one of us had judged the "other."

We all make judgments. It is part of our human nature—part of our sinfulness. We make judgments about what is right and wrong, based on our opinions. We make judgments about what is good or bad, based on our preferences. We make judgments about truth and error, based on our beliefs. But what is worse, we make pre-judgments about other people, based on our experiences—our learned prejudices. Some of us are more sexist, ageist, or racist than others, but there is an "ist" in all of us. There are no exceptions. We are all human.

The reason we do this is that we want to be masters of our own fate, makers of our own destiny. We want to be like God. God is the Judge, and we want to take His place. This is the basis of our salvation—God lovingly took our place because we sinfully took His. But even after God has forgiven us, even after our salvation, we persist in making judgments. We maintain our prejudices. I still tend to judge people by their appearance, their education, or their background. Don't judge me. I am no better or worse than you. We are all sinners.

Brothers and sisters, do not slander one another. Anyone who speaks against a brother or sister or judges them speaks against the law and judges it. When you judge the law, you are not keeping it, but sitting in judgment on it. There is only one Lawgiver and Judge, the one who is able to save and destroy. But you—who are you to judge your neighbor?
(James 4:11-12)

I learned a valuable lesson about my judgment on a trip to the former Yugoslavia in the 1980s. My friends and I had been invited to speak in a church in a small rural community. The regular churchgoers were well-dressed, on time, and courteous—as expected. But after the service started, another group of people arrived. They were travelers who were living on the edge of the community. They were noisy, unkempt, and clearly not used to the religious expectations of the local congregation. There was an immediate tension in the room between the insiders and the outsiders. Everyone started making judgments—including me.

At the end of the service, we invited people who needed prayer to come to the front. All of the travelers wanted us to pray for them. They ran forward with open arms—welcoming us to their community. They were passionate and hungry for change. I didn't expect this response. We laid hands on their matted hair, and many of them went home miraculously healed. I was shocked at their simple faith. Most of the well-dressed churchgoers, on the other hand, stayed in their seats—judging the outsiders. Sadly, not one of them was healed. Judgment is an enemy of faith.

This story was played out in the life of Jesus. The insiders, the religious Pharisees—who were expected to recognize Him and believe His word—were closed and critical. But the outsiders—the Samaritans and the Gentiles, who were not expected to believe or put their hope in Christ—were the ones who saw Him for who He was, and who often went home miraculously healed. Luke records one of these unlikely outsiders—a Roman centurion.

The Centurion

When Jesus had finished saying all this to the people who were listening, he entered Capernaum. There a centurion's servant, whom his master valued highly, was sick and about to die. The centurion heard of Jesus and sent some elders of the Jews to him, asking him to come and heal his servant. When they came to Jesus, they pleaded earnestly with him, "This man deserves to have you do this, because he loves our nation and has built our synagogue." So Jesus went with them. He was not far from the house when the centurion sent friends to say to him: "Lord, don't trouble yourself, for I do not deserve to have you come under my roof. That is why I did not even consider myself worthy to come to you. But say the word, and my servant will be healed. For I myself am a man under authority, with soldiers under me. I tell this one, 'Go,' and he goes; and that one, 'Come,' and he comes. I say to my servant, 'Do this,' and he does it." When Jesus heard this, he was amazed at him, and turning to the crowd following him, he said, "I tell you, I have not found such great faith even in Israel." Then the men who had been sent returned to the house and found the servant well. (Luke 7:1-10)

This centurion lived and served in Capernaum, on the northwest shore of the Sea of Galilee, a community that became the center of Jesus' ministry. I don't think it is coincidental that Jesus chose this part of the world to live. Although the area around Capernaum consisted of several Jewish communities, the province of Galilee as a whole was described as "Galilee of the Gentiles" (see Matthew 4:15). It was a place for outsiders. It was the perfect place for Jesus to reveal His radical and countercultural message.

Although this centurion was respected by many in Capernaum because he loved the nation and had built the synagogue, he was still a representative of the oppressive Roman Empire. As a commander in the Roman army charged with the responsibility of keeping order, handing out punishments, and perhaps even overseeing executions, he was a man to be feared. Not everyone in the community welcomed his presence. He was an outsider in a province of outsiders. A man to be viewed with suspicion.

However, when Jesus heard about the centurion's sick servant, He went to heal him without hesitation. There was no reticence because of the Roman soldier's heritage, no immediate judgment of the Roman Empire's injustices and no thought of His own future suffering at Roman hands. Jesus responded how He always responded—in unmerited love. But this is not "just another miracle" (remarkable as it is); it is also a story of a Gentile with surprising faith, an outsider with insider knowledge. Even Jesus was amazed. It was the beginning of a movement that would overtake the world—and would surprise me two thousand years later in Yugoslavia.

The heart of this story is not the healing of the slave; that's important, because without it the story wouldn't exist, but it's just the framework for what Luke wants to highlight. What matters is the centurion's faith.[21]

(Tom Wright)

Jesus and ...

The healing of the centurion's servant is a great demonstration of love, and a remarkable example of faith, but it is also a lesson in judgment. Jesus didn't just see a Roman centurion; He looked for—and found—a man with faith. He didn't make a judgment on the man's outward appearance (as I had with the travelers in Yugoslavia); He looked at the man's heart. How would I have reacted on that day in Capernaum? How would you have reacted? How should we react?

Aspects of faith

Luke's narrative of the centurion contains several potential viewpoints: the perspectives of the community in general, the other Roman soldiers, the Jewish elders, the sick servant, the centurion's friends, and of course, Jesus Christ Himself. Each of these potential viewpoints can teach us about our reactions, our judgments—even our prejudices. They can also teach us about how we look for and discover faith in the most unlikely circumstances.

To understand the community reaction, we need to remember that the centurion was a Roman soldier. The average member of the community in first-century Israel would have reacted to soldiers as we do today with a mixture of respect and disquiet. This became evident to me when watching a state ceremony in England. The pageantry and spectacle were extraordinary, the presentation and precision of the marching soldiers was awe-inspiring, but the weapons they carried were real: they were trained to kill.

When the inhabitants of Capernaum saw the centurion, they would have seen the armor he wore and the sword by his side. They would have observed the authority with which he commanded his men, and the discipline they maintained. They were meant to see them. A parade of soldiers is designed to catch our attention, to communicate power, and in the case of an occupying force, to engender terror. The community respected the centurion's open hand and yet feared his closed fist. This is the tension with which the local people in Galilee lived, and into which Jesus walked.

Jesus, however, didn't perceive the way we do. He didn't focus on the externals. He didn't focus on outward appearance. He fixed His eyes on the eternal, not the temporal. He was looking for faith on the earth, as He always will, and He found it in a Roman soldier. Where the community saw a threatening uniform, Jesus saw an open heart. If we are going to learn from this story, we must grasp that we are not chosen by God because of our outward appearance. Faith is of the heart.

But the Lord said to Samuel, "Do not consider his appearance or his height, for I have rejected him. The Lord does not look at the things people look at. People look at the outward appearance, but the Lord looks at the heart. (1 Samuel 16:7)

But we are not valued by God because of our authority. Jesus didn't respond to this man because of his rank, but because of his faith. Faith is open to every one of us—whatever our position.

There are other viewpoints in this story that are worth considering here. Luke's account doesn't record how many men the centurion commanded, but his sentry might have consisted of fifty to eighty soldiers. How did these legionaries view their commander? I suspect that their primary concern was his rank. He was important and they were not. They would have wanted what he had. They believed, as many of us do, that the pathway to recognition is promotion.

We often think that our position in our family, company, or society makes us significant. But we are not valued by God because of our authority. Jesus didn't respond to this man because of his rank, but because of his faith. Faith is open to every one of us—whatever our position.

For it is with your heart that you believe and are justified, and it is with your mouth that you profess your faith and are saved. As Scripture says, "Anyone who believes in him will never be put to shame." For there is no difference between Jew and Gentile—the same Lord is Lord of all and richly blesses all who call on him, for, "Everyone who calls on the name of the Lord will be saved." (Romans 10:10–13)

What about the Jewish elders? What was their view of this centurion? They evidently respected his love for the nation and his generosity in building their synagogue. They saw his compassion for his servant, and his humility in how he responded to Jesus. They saw him as a good successful man, a man who deserved a miracle, just as I saw the "respectable" churchgoers in Yugoslavia. But do any of us deserve a miracle?

Grace, by definition, is unmerited. Thankfully, God's mercy *doesn't* give us what we *do* deserve, and amazingly, God's grace *does* give us what we *don't* deserve. The centurion didn't—and couldn't—earn a miracle for his servant. We are not saved by God because of our achievements, our education, or our background. Faith is a God-given grace.

For it is by grace you have been saved, through faith—and this is not from yourselves, it is the gift of God—not by works, so that no one can boast. (Ephesians 2:8-9)

Of course, there are many unanswered questions in this passage. For example, did the centurion have a family? Why did he value his servant so much? Who were his friends (who are not even mentioned in Matthew's account)? Although we don't know, it seems that Jesus was more amazed by the centurion's faith than his commendable relationships. We are not included in Christ because of our associations, our family, or our heritage. We are children of Abraham by faith. Faith is spiritual and personal.

> **In other words, it is not the children by physical descent who are God's children, but it is the children of the promise who are regarded as Abraham's offspring.**
>
> (Romans 9:8)

By placing ourselves in the shoes of the characters in this story, we can explore the different perspectives we can have, and judgments we can make. Each of these judgments can prevent us from perceiving the truth. So which one of these characters are we most like? Do we have the same faith as the centurion? Do we have the ability to perceive faith as Jesus did in this story, or as Paul did in Lystra?

> **In Lystra there sat a man who was lame. He had been that way from birth and had never walked. He listened to Paul as he was speaking. Paul looked directly at him, saw that he had faith to be healed and called out, "Stand up on your feet!" At that, the man jumped up and began to walk.** (Acts 14:8–10)

The centurion's faith

To take our exploration of faith further, we need to consider the extraordinary response of the centurion. On hearing that Jesus was on His way, he sent a message to say that there was no need to come to his house. Instead, he asked Jesus to "say the word, and my servant will be healed" (Luke 7:7). It was this statement that revealed the centurion's faith, which amazed Jesus. His confession reveals four ideas about faith, which I want to highlight and from which we all can learn.

First, the centurion knew that when he gave a command to his soldiers or servants, they would obey him—not just because he *had* authority, but because he was "*under* authority" (Luke 7:8). He understood that his right to command came from his submission to his own commanders, and ultimately the Roman Emperor. He identified this same principle in the life of Jesus. He believed that Jesus had the right to command because He was under the authority of God Himself. But how did he know this? Was it a revelation from God or was it because he had met other commanders before?

Many years ago, I was in a queue of people who were boarding a ferry. In front of me, a tall man wearing a gray suit caught my attention. Even though I never saw his face, I immediately wanted to follow him, which I did. He had an air of authority about him. I discovered later that he was a general in the armed forces. I wonder whether the centurion was captivated by a similar compulsion to follow Christ, just as the disciples had been. Either way, the centurion's faith was based on Jesus Christ Himself and who he believed Him to be. This, of course, is the foundation for our faith as well.

Once the centurion had settled in his heart that Jesus was sent from God, he reveals another aspect of faith—our second idea. He asked Him to speak. He knew that even with his own limited authority, when he said "go," soldiers went. So he believed that when Jesus said "go," sickness went. He didn't need Jesus to come to his house, or lay hands on his servant. He knew that Jesus just had to "say the word." He believed the speaking was significant.

This faith is not abstract belief about God, or the learning of dogmas. It is simple, clear belief that when Jesus commands that something be done, it will be done. He regards Jesus like a military officer, with authority over sickness and health. If Jesus says that someone is to get well, they will. What could be simpler?[22]

(Tom Wright)

His simple faith is a challenge to all of us. Are we prepared to take Jesus at His word as the centurion did, or as the royal official did when he begged Jesus to heal his son (see John 4:50)? Are we prepared to believe the word, as Abraham did when God promised him a son (see Romans 4:18–21)? Are we prepared to obey the word, as Jesus expected the disciples to do when He gave them the great commission?

In this commission, Jesus first established His right to command, and then He spoke the command itself, "Go and make disciples." The authority and the command were connected. Our faith is not only based on who we believe Jesus is but also whether we believe what He says. The centurion understood both Jesus' authority to command and the power of the command itself. Do we have the same understanding? Do we respond as readily as he did?

Then Jesus came to them and said, "All authority in heaven and on earth has been given to me. Therefore go and make disciples of all nations, baptizing them in the name of the Father and of the Son and of the Holy Spirit, and teaching them to obey everything I have commanded you. And surely I am with you always, to the very end of the age. (Matthew 28:18-20)

Interestingly, we are not told how the centurion accessed his faith in the first place. However, there is a small clue in Luke's narrative, which highlights our third idea. It says, "The centurion heard of Jesus" (Luke 7:3). The hearing is significant. In the book of Romans, Paul the apostle explains that we receive faith when we hear the message, the gospel of the Lord Jesus Christ, or "the word about Christ," as Paul puts it (Romans 10:17). The Greek word he used (*rhema*) usually refers to the spoken word.

The Centurion

> As we hear the truth, our ears become our eyes, and we are enabled to see.

I suspect that the centurion had heard more than we read about in this story. Either way, he believed enough about what he had heard to ask Jesus to come.

During the ministry of Jesus Christ, bodies were healed, people were liberated, and lives were changed by a single spoken word. This is the creative and transformative power that is also in play when the gospel is proclaimed, when the message is heard, when the word of God is spoken.

Something mysterious and miraculous takes place every time a sermon is preached. Faith comes and our hearts are opened. As we hear the truth, our ears become our eyes, and we are enabled to see. I believe this is what happened to the centurion, and I know this is what can happen to each one of us. If we put ourselves in the position where we can hear the message, faith will come.

Consequently, faith comes from hearing the message, and the message is heard through the word about Christ.

(Romans 10:17)

&

Jesus and ...

So far, I have used the story of the centurion to highlight three ideas about faith. The centurion placed his trust in Jesus, understood the power of confession, and received faith from hearing the message about Christ. In other words, our faith is dependent on who we believe in our heart, what we say with our mouth, and what we hear of the message. The fourth idea is highlighted by the centurion's response: he acted on his faith. Faith is an entrustment. What are we going to do with it? How are we going to act on it?

Jesus and us

It is very easy to study a story, hear a message, or even read a book—and walk away completely unchanged. I know—I have done it many times. But at the very least, the story of the centurion should give us hope for change.

Here was a man who would have had a typically pagan upbringing, yet didn't allow his background to rob him of the possibility of a miracle. He lived in challenging times, yet didn't let them take his hope. He wasn't expected to believe, yet he did. He may not have had as much faith as he thought he needed, yet he had enough to call for Jesus. And then, one word from Jesus was sufficient to heal his servant and change his life.

As we read the centurion's story, we might think like the elders—in terms of "deserving" a miracle. Or we may recognize the same judgments in ourselves as were held by the community at large. Or we may simply see ourselves in the sick servant, a person desperately in need of help. Wherever we find ourselves in the story, whatever our perspective, let's follow the centurion's example and make a decision to call on the name of the Lord Jesus Christ.

> As Scripture says, "Anyone who believes in him will never be put to shame." For there is no difference between Jew and Gentile—the same Lord is Lord of all and richly blesses all who call on him, for, "Everyone who calls on the name of the Lord will be saved."
>
> (Romans 10:11-13)

Jesus and ...

QUESTIONS TO CONSIDER

1. The Roman centurion would have been judged because of his uniform and his military manner (Luke 7:8). In what circumstances have you misjudged someone because of their outward appearance (1 Samuel 16:7)?

2. Prior to the story of the centurion (Luke 7:1-10), Jesus challenged His disciples about their tendency to judge people (Luke 6:37-42). What steps did He require them to take?

3. The elders in this story believed that the centurion deserved a miracle (Luke 7:4-5). Are there any circumstances, apart from our faith or lack of it, which attract or hinder the miraculous in our lives (Mark 6:1-6)?

4. Jesus perceived faith in the centurion (Luke 7:9) and Paul saw faith in the man from Lystra (Acts 14:9). How do we see the unseen (John 3:3; Ephesians 1:18; 2 Corinthians 4:18; Hebrews 11:1-3)?

5. The centurion's servant was healed and yet it was the centurion who had faith (Luke 7:9-10). How do we explain this (John 11:38-43)?

6. God has given each of us a measure of faith (Romans 12:3), yet most of us think we need more (Mark 9:24). Is it possible to increase our faith (Luke 17:5; Romans 10:17)?

7. The centurion recognized the authority and power of Jesus Christ (Luke 7:6-8). What is the difference between authority and power (Luke 9:1)? Is it possible to have one without the other (Matthew 28:18-20; Acts 1:8)?

8. How do we balance the facts of our challenging circumstances with our faith in the promises of God (Romans 4:18-21)?

9. The centurion's faith was rewarded (Luke 7:9-10), but what if we don't see the reward (Hebrews 11:39-40)? How do we maintain our faith in God if our prayers seem to remain unanswered (Daniel 3:16-18)?

10. What has been your main takeaway from this chapter? What lesson have you learned that you can apply to your life today?

And now these three remain: faith, hope and love. But the greatest of these is love.

1 Corinthians 13:13

155

CONCLUSION

&

Jesus and ...

Luke's gospel is a storybook

Although the Lord Jesus Christ is the central Character in the story, there are many other stories of remarkable men and women who play significant roles in the narrative. In this book, I chose five of these minor characters to study in order to focus on five essential needs in our lives.

The stories of the centurion, Zechariah's family, and the man with leprosy reveal our need of *faith*, *hope*, and *love*, respectively. This triad of truths are foundational if we are going to live the life that God wants each one of us to live.

And now these three remain: faith, hope and love. But the greatest of these is love. (1 Corinthians 13:13)

The subjects of the other two stories may seem less important, yet John the Baptist's story of *purpose* and Anna's story of *significance* contain fundamental revelations that are also essential to a fulfilled life. It is these two ideas that enable us to make the most of each day and make the most of our lives.

Conclusion

> ### And we know that in all things God works for the good of those who love him, who have been called according to his purpose.
> (Romans 8:28)

Of course, as you read this book, you will have realized that I have only scratched the surface. There are many other truths to be found in these five stories, and also many other stories to be found in Luke's gospel. May I therefore encourage you not only to reread the stories but also read the entire gospel.

When my brother was an atheist, my wife and I gave him a novel about Luke. He was so captivated by the story that he read Luke's gospel. In it he discovered the central Character of the story, the Lord Jesus Christ, and like the minor characters in the gospel, he found faith and purpose at the feet of Jesus.

It is my profound desire that after reading this book, you will do the same.

The story of ... Luke is the story of every man's pilgrimage through despair and life-darkness, through suffering and anguish, through bitterness and sorrow, through doubt and cynicism, through rebellion and hopelessness to the feet and the understanding of God.[23] (Taylor Caldwell)

REFERENCES

[1] C. S. Lewis. *The Screwtape Letters.* Fount. 1942. 1977. P.126.

[2] E. M. Bounds. *The Complete Works of E. M. Bounds on Prayer.* Baker Book House. 1990. Book 7. *Power through Prayer.* P.447.

[3] Colton Wickramaratne. *My Adventure in Faith.* Onward Books. 2007. P.224.

[4] Tom Wright. *Luke for Everyone.* SPCK. 2001. 2014. P.2

[5] William Shakespeare. *Romeo and Juliet.* Act 2. Scene 2. Line 43.

[6] Frederick Buechner. In Brennan Manning. *Reflections for Ragamuffins.* Harper. 1998. P. 117.

[7] George Elliot. *Middlemarch.* Penguin. 1871. 2003. P.838.

[8] Anonymous. Inscription on a sundial. In Oswald Sanders. *Spiritual Leadership.* Moody Press. 1994. P.95.

[9] Ken Robinson. *The Element.* Penguin Group. 2009.

[10] Mihaly Csikszentmihalyi. *Flow.* Harper & Row. 1990.

[11] Joel Nederhood. In Samuel T. Logan. Ed. *The Preacher and Preaching.* Presbyterian and Reformed Publishing Company. 1986. P.34

[12] Amelia Taylor (mother of James Hudson Taylor). In Dr and Mrs Howard Taylor. *Biography of James Hudson Taylor.* Hodder and Stoughton. 1973. P.22–23.

[13] Billy Graham. In Benjamin K. Forrest, Kevin L. King, Bill Curtis, and Dwayne Milioni. *A Legacy of Preaching Volume 2*. Zondervan. 2018. P. 451.

[14] Tom Wright. *God and the Pandemic*. SPCK. 2020. P.3.

[15] Neil White. *The Sanctuary of Outcasts*. Murdoch Books. 2009. P.20.

[16] King Baldwin IV. In Simon Sebag Montefiore. *Jerusalem: The Biography*. Weideneld & Nicolson. 2011. P.244.

[17] *Moravian Church Archives*. Bethlehem, Pa. Issue 84. December 2013.

[18] Scot McKnight. *The Jesus Creed*. Paraclete Press. 2014. P.159.

[19] Stephen Grosz. *The Examined Life*. Chatto and Windus. 2013. P.26.

[20] Neil White. *In the Sanctuary of Outcasts*. Murdoch Books. 2009. P.281.

[21] Tom Wright. *Luke for Everyone*. SPCK. 2001. 2014. P.80.

[22] Tom Wright. *Luke for Everyone*. SPCK. 2001. 2014. P.80–81.

[23] Taylor Caldwell. *Dear and Glorious Physician*. Collins. 1959. 1960. P.5.

ROBERT FERGUSSON

Robert Fergusson, internationally recognized
Hillsong Church teacher, is the author of two books, including
Are You Getting This? and *Making Connections That Work*.
Robert is one of the key team members at Hillsong Church,
where he has been on staff for over thirty years. He is passionate
about imparting practical life principles from the Bible, and his
primary responsibilities involve pastoral oversight and preaching
and teaching. Robert is married to Amanda; they have three adult
children and currently seven grandchildren.